A FIRST FRENCH

This elementary course in the French language has been de-
signed for young readers and adult beginners alike, to enable
them to acquire a working knowledge of modern idiomatic
French which they can put to use in a variety of practical
situations. It is divided into a series of graded lessons, each
covering one or two important aspects of French, so that
the reader can work his way through the course with ease.
Exercises are included at the end of each lesson, the answers
to which are given in Part II of the book.

D0332587

KS

A FIRST
FRENCH

N. Scarlyn Wilson, M.A.

Illustrated by
Gordon Stowell

TEACH YOURSELF BOOKS
Hodder and Stoughton

First printed in this series 1968
Seventeenth impression 1986

Copyright © 1962
Hodder and Stoughton Ltd

All rights reserved. No part of this publication may be repro-
duced or transmitted in any form or by any means, electronic
or mechanical, including photocopy, recording, or any infor-
mation storage and retrieval system, without permission in
writing from the publisher.

ISBN 0 340 26418 7

Printed in Great Britain
for Hodder and Stoughton Educational
a division of Hodder and Stoughton Ltd,
Mill Road, Dunton Green, Sevenoaks, Kent
by Richard Clay (The Chaucer Press) Ltd, Bungay, Suffolk

CONTENTS

PART II

TO BEGIN WITH . . .

There's a story—probably not true, but never mind—
that one man offered to teach another a thousand French
words for £5. The second man reckoned that if he knew a
thousand French words he'd be able to get along very well
when he went to France for his holidays, so he agreed.
"Now," said the first man, "a lot of English words end in
'-tion'." The other nodded. "Yes, heaps of them, 'direc-
tion', 'sensation'—oh, and many more. What about them?"
"Well," answered the first man, "there are over a thousand
of them, and they are exactly the same in French as they are
in English." With which he pocketed the £5 note and walked
off.

Of course what he said was largely true. Hundreds of
words do end in "-tion". You might even find a thousand
if you searched through a big dictionary, and most of them
are the same in French as in English. Now it may be
pleasant to discover that you know the French for "multipli-
cation" without having to learn it, but you wouldn't get on
very well in France if the only French words you knew were
ones like "pre-combustion" or "ratiocination"! Certainly
it's useful to know as many words as possible, whether in
your own language or in another, but obviously we want
first to know the ordinary words, the ones we use often. In
this book the total number of French words to be found in
the exercises is under five hundred. While single words are
important, it's far more important to be able to combine
them with others, so that you can express different ideas
by stringing much the same words together in various
ways. There's a great difference between "I will give
you two pounds" and "you will give me two pounds", yet
each sentence contains almost the same words. So in
this book we begin from the first to use words together
so that we can form them into simple but complete
sentences.

This book, by the way, belongs to the same family as that very famous book *Teach Yourself French.*.

This present book does not cover so much ground as the earlier one and takes it more slowly, but it's planned in the same way.

Each lesson deals with one or two different things to be learned, beginning with the simplest and leading on in the next one to something more difficult.

If you read the explanations carefully and study the examples given to illustrate the rules explained you should be able to tackle the exercises in each lesson easily enough. Some people grasp things very quickly, but if they rush ahead too fast they may forget something they had learnt earlier. The best thing to do is to go along at the pace that suits you, and not as if you were being rocketed into outer space! You're teaching yourself French, not going into orbit round the earth! So make sure you've really understood one lesson before you go on to the next, and don't forget to refer back to an earlier page as you work through the book.

In Part II of this book you will find the answers to the exercises in Part I. Now, some people reading a thriller get so worked up that they can't resist turning to the last page when they're only half-way through it to see how it ends. There's no particular reason why they shouldn't, but it's not really fair to the author, and it spoils the reader's fun. In short, Part II isn't intended to be used as a crib, but to check whether what you've written is right. So don't turn to it while you're doing an exercise unless you're really stumped. Have a bet with yourself, so to speak, and then turn to Part II to find out whether you've won or lost. You won't have to pay yourself anything either way! You may find you need some extra practice, especially when you're revising earlier lessons. You can get it by doing the exercise in Part II and then checking whether you're right by using the exercise in Part I this time as the "key".

To make a change from exercises you'll find at the end of each lesson a "Have a Try" piece. They're not difficult.

With a bit of luck, a bit of intelligent guessing and, if necessary, some help from someone else, if you can get it ("Oh! don't bother me! Can't you see I'm busy!"), you should be able to get the general sense of most of them. Well, that's all. Now, "Have a Try"!

HOW TO PRONOUNCE FRENCH

French is not just something you have to learn at school. It is a living language spoken by well over forty million people in France, some of them living little more than twenty miles from the English coast. We need therefore to know how to pronounce French as well as we can.

The best way to do this, of course, is to hear it spoken either by French people or by others with a good knowledge of the language. It is, in consequence, a good idea to tune into French radio stations or to listen to B.B.C. broadcasts in French. In this book we can do no more than give a few hints. They are no substitute for hearing French spoken by French people.

Do not (REPEAT NOT) try to master the Notes which follow at one go. They are merely a rough guide for reference.

A dozen or more letters of the alphabet sound the same in French as in English. But there are one or two consonants we must be careful about.

c sounds like *k* when followed by *a, o* or *u*; for instance *café*, coffee, *cour*, court or *curieux*, curious.

c is softened when it is followed by *e* or *i*: *certain*, certain; *cité*, city.

g followed by *a, o, u* has the hard sound as in "gate", "goat" or "gutter".
Examples in French *gaz*, gas; *gorge*, gorge; and *guide*, guide.

g followed by *e* or *i* is soft; softer in fact than in English: *général*, general; *girafe*, giraffe.

j sounds like the "s" in "*pleasure*" or "*treasure*": *je*, I; *juge*, judge.

s often has the hissing sound as in the English "*stiff*", but between two vowels it is much more like our "z": *maison*, house.

h is often "mute", that is, not pronounced at all as in

hôtel, hotel. Even when it is not "mute" it is never pronounced as strongly as in English.

Vowels

a This may sound like the "a" in English "mat": *avoir*, to have. Or it may sound like "a" in English "father": *a*, has; *arbre*, tree. It never rhymes with the English *same*.

e This may rhyme with the English "cur": *de*, of, from.

é with this accent (acute) is something like the English sound of *surprise* "eh?"—but cut off short.

è with a "grave" accent is longer and rhymes with the English "there" or "chair".

i This mostly has the sound of *ee* in the English "been". For instance *il*, he, sounds like the English "eel" said quickly. *i* in French never has the sound of the English "fire" or "higher".

o Usually sounds like the *oa* in English "goat".

u This is not like the English "u". If you say "huge", making your lips into as small a round as possible, you get somewhere near it.

Often we get two or more vowels together. For instance:

au— something like the "o" in English "low".

eau—similar in sound.

ou— sounds rather like the "o" in "who".

Silent Letters

Sometimes letters at the end of a word in French are not pronounced at all.

Such are, often, *e, es* and *ent*.

On the other hand, if a word ends in an *s* and the next word begins with a vowel (a, e, i, o, u) the French, softening the "s" into a "z" sound, bunch the two words together.

For instance, *les idées* (the ideas) would be run into one in speaking, and would sound a little (not very!) like "lazy day" in English.

AGAIN a lot of endings of words in French sound rather (but not exactly) like one another: the sound being roughly like that of the "a" in "day" or "may".

Such are the endings: *-er, -é, -ais, -ait, ez*, all of which we shall meet often.

FINALLY, there are a lot of sounds in French which do not rhyme with any English word. They are nasal sounds because to some extent they are made by speaking, as we say, "through the nose". Something, but not very like it, are the English words "sang" or "bang" said "through the nose" with the "g" cut off short.

We shall meet this sound in French words such as *vin*, wine; *main*, hand. It is not difficult to imitate, but we have nothing really like it in English. So, again, try to listen to some real French on records or on the radio, even if you don't understand what is being said.

At best, what has been said above can be no more than a very rough guide.

LESSON ONE

HOW TO SAY "THE" AND "A"

In English a noun—that is a word such as man, horse or table—a word which denotes a person or thing—is said to be masculine when it refers to a male being and feminine when it refers to a female being. So, man, boy, soldier are masculine nouns, and woman, girl and actress are feminine nouns. We should refer to any of the first three as "he" and to any of the second three as "she". But when we come across a noun which denotes, not a person, but a thing such as table or motor-car, we refer to it as "it".

In French it is different. Every noun in French must be either masculine or feminine. There is no third choice. In other words, any noun, including those denoting things, must be either masculine or feminine. In English we can put "the" before any noun, person or thing, whether we are talking about one person or thing only (in which case we say the noun is in the singular) or whether we are referring to more than one (in which case we say the noun is in the plural). When we use "a" instead of "the" the only change we can make is to alter "a" into "an" when the next word begins with one of the vowels a, e, i, o or u, and we do this only because it's easier to say. So we have: a house, an officer, the bull (singular), the cows (plural) and so on.

But in French the words for "the" and "a" do not always remain the same. They must "agree" with the noun they come before. If the noun is masculine the "the" must be masculine as well, while if the noun is feminine, then "the" must be feminine too.

"The" in French has the following forms: *le, la, l'* and *les.*

Le is used before any masculine singular noun except one beginning with a vowel or a mute (unpronounced) "h".

le soldat, the soldier   *le garçon*,[1] the boy (*also* the waiter)
le jardin, the garden   *le magasin*, the shop

La is used before any feminine singular noun except one beginning with a vowel or mute "h".

la femme, the woman (*or* the wife)   *la fille*, the girl (*or* daughter)
la maison, the house   *la porte*, the door

L' is used before any singular noun, masculine or feminine, which begins with a vowel or mute "h".

l'homme, the man (*masc.*)   *l'hôtel*, hotel (*masc.*)
l'arbre, the tree (*masc.*)   *l'actrice*, actress (*fem.*)

The reason for this is simply that *le officier* (the officer) or *la église* (the church) would sound rather ugly, so the *e* and *a* are dropped from *le* and *la* in these cases and the two words are pronounced as one: *l'officier* (masc.) and *l'église* (fem.).

Les is used before any plural noun, whether masculine or feminine.

In English we make a word plural by adding an "s" to the singular. The French do the same: so we have *le garçon* (sing.), *les garçons* (pl.) (boys). But remember that *les* is used as the plural not only of *le* but also of *la*.

la vache, les vaches, cow(s)   *l'hôtel, les hôtels*, hotel(s)
l'arbre (masc.), *les arbres*, tree(s)   *l'actrice, les actrices*, actress(es)

"A" or "An"

"A" or "an" before a masculine singular noun is *un*.

"A" or "an" before a feminine singular noun is *une*.

un mouton, a sheep   *un fleuve*, a (big) river
une ville, a town   *une rue*, a street

How do we know whether a French word is masculine or feminine?

The plain truth is that we can't always be sure. A noun

---

[1] The mark under the "c" in *garçon* means that the "c" sounds like the "c" in "centre" or "city". Without it, the "c" would sound like the "c" in "coke" or "caterpillar".

denoting a male being, such as a king or a sailor, is, of course, likely to be masculine, while a word such as "queen" or "aunt" is obviously feminine. But when we come to things there is little to guide us. The only thing to do, therefore, when we come across a new word is to get into the way of learning not only the word but also the form of "the" which goes with it: for instance, not just *champ*—but *le champ* (the) field. This has given us a start, so now we can practise what we have learnt so far. But first a short list of words we shall need if we are to be able, even in this first lesson, to write real sentences.

Word List 1

il, he	*à*, to, in, at
elle, she	*de*, of, from
ils, they (*masc.*)	*avec*, with
elles, they (*fem.*)	*et*, and
est, is	*dans*, in, into
sont, are	*derrière*, behind
où, where	*qui*, who, which

(Both *est* (is) and *et* (and) sound the same, like the "a" in "day".)

Exercise 1 (*a*)

Put into English:

1. Le garçon est dans le jardin. 2. L'actrice est à la porte de la maison. 3. Où est le soldat? Il est à l'hôtel. 4. Où est la femme? Elle est à l'église. 5. Les garçons sont dans la rue. 6. Une vache et un mouton sont dans le jardin derrière la maison. 7. L'homme qui est à l'hôtel est un officier. 8. Où sont les vaches? Elles sont dans le champ derrière l'église. 9. L'actrice qui est dans la rue est la femme de l'officier. 10. Un soldat est à la porte de l'hôtel avec une femme qui est la fille d'une actrice.

Exercise 1 (*b*)

Put into French:

1. The boy is behind a tree in the garden. 2. The officer is with the soldiers in the street. 3. Where are the girls? They are in the house. 4. Where are the sheep? They are in the field behind the hotel. 5. The daughters of the actress are in

the church. 6. The waiter is at the door of the hotel. 7. The wife of the officer is in the street. 8. Where are the soldiers? They are in the field with the officer. 9. A cow and a sheep are in the garden. 10. The woman who is at the door of the church is the daughter of the actress. 11. The man and the woman are in the fields. 12. Where is the cow? It (she) is in the garden.

You will not know all the words in the following passage, but you should be able to guess most of them.

Have a Try 1

Le lion est un animal dangereux. Dans le jardin zoologique à Paris et à Londres il est dans une cage. Le spectateur est derrière une barrière. L'hippopotame—une créature extraordinaire—est content, mais (*but*) pour le tigre et le léopard la captivité est peut-être (*perhaps*) cruelle.

LESSON TWO

HOW TO USE WORDS SUCH AS "GOOD" "BAD", "LARGE" AND "SMALL"

If you say "I met a man" all we know about him is that he is grown-up. That would not be much help to the police, for instance, in tracing a burglar. The man may be tall or short, young or old, rich or poor, as bald as an egg or as fat as a prize pig. The words which tell us something particular about a person or thing are known as adjectives. We needn't bother much about that: it's just one of the things we have to learn to accept (like the mumps!). The point is that we constantly need such words to make our meaning clearer, and therefore have to know how to use them. In English the form of these words never alters: a great man, a great city, great crowds—it's always the same.

Now we saw in the last lesson that the French word for "the" alters; it has to be masculine or feminine, singular or plural to match the noun it goes with. It's exactly the same with "big", "small" and the rest of them. Each must "agree" with the noun it refers to. Thus, *le grand roi*, the great king. But if we want to say "the great queen" then, as *la reine* (queen) is feminine, *grand* must be feminine to agree with it. How is this to be done?

General Rule: To make an adjective feminine, add an *e* to the masculine:

haut, haute, high	*grand, grande*, great (large)
joli, jolie, pretty (nice)	*petit, petite*, small (little)

BUT

I. If the adjective already ends in an *e* make no change.

jeune, young   *la jeune fille*, the young girl

II. If the adjective ends in *-en* or *-on* double the *n* and add *e*.

italien(ne), Italian   *bon(ne)*, good

5

III. NOTE, however, that the feminine of *vieux* (old) is *vieille:* of *beau* (beautiful), *belle*, and of *long* (long), *longue*.

une vieille femme, an old woman   *la belle maison,* the fine house
une longue rue, a long street

Any adjective has to agree with its noun even when it does not come next to it: *la maison est petite*.

Some nouns, by the way, can be made feminine by adding an *e* :

un ami, a (boy) friend   *une amie,* a (girl) friend
un cousin, une cousine, a cousin

We saw in the first lesson that in French as in English the most usual way to make a noun plural is to add an -*s* to the singular. It is the same with adjectives.

un bon livre, a good book   *une belle église,* a beautiful church
les bons livres, the good books *les belles actrices,* the beautiful
                                                   actresses

How to Say "I am", "We are", "You are"

We know already *il est*, he is, and *ils sont*, they are. Here is what we call the "Present" of "to be" in full.

Singular	*Plural*
1st Person *je suis*, I am	*nous sommes*, we are
2nd Person (*tu es*), (thou art)	*vous êtes*, you are
3rd Person *il* (*elle*) *est*, he (she) is	*ils* (*elles*) *sont*, they are

We never use "thou art" in modern English. We say "you" whether we are talking to one person or to several. The French use *tu* only when talking to members of their own family or to very close friends, so we shan't really need it in this book.

Now for Some Practice

Word List 2

mais, but	*sur,* on
très, very	*la chambre,* the room
un(e), one	*la voiture,* the (motor) car (*also* (railway) coach)
deux, two	*ici,* here
trois, three	*devant,* before, in front of
la table, the table	*le lit,* bed

Exercise 2 (*a*)

Put into English:

1. La voiture est vieille, mais elle est bonne. 2. La petite fille de l'actrice est dans le jardin avec deux amis. 3. Les livres qui sont sur la table dans la chambre de la vieille femme sont très bons. 4. Les trois filles de la reine sont dans une belle voiture devant la grande église. 5. La chambre où nous sommes est très haute. 6. Où sont les deux petites cousines de l'officier? Elles sont dans le champ derrière l'hôtel. 7. Je suis devant la porte de la maison avec deux amis. 8. Nous sommes dans une jolie maison qui est très

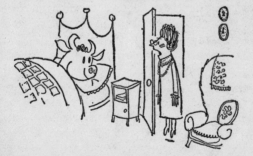

vieille. 9. Les arbres dans le champ où sont les deux petits moutons sont très hauts. 10. Où est la vache? Dans le champ? Elle est sur le lit dans la chambre de la vieille femme!

Exercise 2 (b)

Put into French:

1. We are at a nice (pretty) hotel in the town. 2. The hotel
is old, but the rooms are good. 3. The street in front of the
house where we are is long. 4. Where are the sheep? They
are behind the big trees in the field. 5. Two men, three little
boys and an old woman are in the car. 6. The two little
cousins (*fem.*) of the actress are here. The house where they[1]
are is beautiful. 7. The beds in the rooms at the hotel are
very small. 8. The daughter of the officer and a (boy) friend
are in the street behind the old church. 9. The books which
are on the little table behind the door are good. 10. The
houses in the street are small but they are handsome
(beautiful).

Have a Try 2

Il est évident que (*that*) les vaches et les moutons sont
stupides, mais je suis certain que l'éléphant est un animal
très intelligent. Dans un jardin zoologique et dans un cirque
il est docile (*gentle*), mais il est préférable d'observer (*to
observe*) les éléphants dans les excellents films en couleurs où
les bêtes sauvages sont en liberté parmi (*among*) les fleuves,
les fôrets et les plaines de l'Afrique ou de l'Inde.

[1] "They". Watch out!

LESSON THREE

HOW TO MAKE WORDS PLURAL

We know that *le garçon* is "the boy" and that "the boys" is *les garçons*. From this we got the general rule that in French, as in English, the usual way to make a word plural is simply to add an *-s* to it. But there are one or two special rules. Here they are:

I. If the word ends in *-s*, *-x* or *-z* make no change. _____ ①

> *le palais, les palais*, the palace(s)
> *la voix, les voix*, the voice(s)
> *le nez, les nez*, the nose(s)

II. If the word ends in *-au* or *-eu* add *-x* NOT *-s*. _____ ②

> *le bateau, les bateaux*, the boat(s)
> *l'eau* (fem.), *les eaux*, the water(s)
> *le cheveu, les cheveux*, the hair(s)

III. If the word ends in *-al* change *-al* into *-aux*. _____ ③

> *le cheval, les chevaux*, the horse(s)
> *le journal, les journaux*, the newspaper(s)

How to Say "I have", "We have"

In the last lesson we saw how to put "I am", "we are" and so on into French. We shall need, at least as often, to be able to use "I have", so here is what is known as the Present Tense of "to have".

Singular	Plural
1st Person *j'ai*,[1] I have	*Nous avons*, we have
2nd Person (*tu as*), (thou hast)	*vous avez*, you have
3rd Person *il* (*elle*), *a*, he (she) has	*ils* (*elles*) *ont*, they have

How to Ask a Question

In English we can ask a question by changing, for instance, "you have" into "have you"? We can do the same in

[1] *Je* (like *le*) is shortened to *j'* when followed by *a, e, i, o* or *u*.

9

French, the only difference being that when we switch the words round we put a dash - (hyphen is the grammar-book name for it) between the two, just to show that even though the "you" (*vous*) is not in its usual place, it is still attached to the "have" by a kind of tow-rope and not to be separated from it.

> "Have you?", *avez-vous?*
> "He (she) is", *il (elle) est*; is he (she)?, *est-il (elle)?*

You should pronounce the *t* in *est-il (elle)?*, running the two words into one, as it sounds better.

How to Say "belongs to"

> *Il est à Paris* and *ils sont à Paris* mean, of course, "He is (they are) in Paris".

BUT *est* followed by *à* can also mean "belongs to" and *sont à*, in the same way, can mean "belong to".

> *Les livres sont à la petite fille.*
> The books belong to the little girl.

Word List 3

le cadeau, the present	*entre*, between
le bois, the wood	*oui*, yes
le fils, the son	*non*, no
le château, the castle	*méchant*, naughty, wicked
le fermier, the farmer	*riche*, rich
la fermière, the farmer's wife	*pauvre*, poor
autre, other	*sûr*, sure
une école, a school	*que*, which, that
profond, deep	*quand*, when
pour, for	

Exercise 3 (*a*)

Put into English:

1. Avez-vous un cadeau pour le petit fils de la fermière? 2. Non. Il est très méchant. Quand les autres garçons sont à l'école il est dans le bois. 3. Les deux grandes voitures qui

sont devant l'hôtel sont à l'officier: il est très riche. 4. Où
sont les deux fils de la jeune actrice? 5. Ils sont sur le fleuve
dans un bateau: l'eau est très profonde. 6. L'actrice qui est à
l'hôtel avec deux amies a une belle voix. 7. Où est le palais
de la reine? Elle a un palais à Londres et un château à
Windsor. 8. Où sont les journaux? Ils sont sur la petite
table. 9. Les deux chevaux et les vieilles vaches qui sont
dans le champ entre la rue et le fleuve sont à la fermière.
10. Nous sommes sûrs que les cadeaux dans la chambre de
l'actrice sont pour nous.

Exercise 3 (b)

Put into French:

1. The great house which is in the field behind the hotel
belongs to the queen. 2. Are you sure that she is here? Yes.
She is at the church. 3. The two soldiers who are in the
street have a small car, but the fine horse in the field belongs
to the officer. 4. We are sure that the old cows and the three
sheep belong to the farmer's wife. 5. Are they at (the)
school? No. They are in the woods. 6. The rooms in the
castle are very big. 7. The sons of the actress are on the
river with the other boys. 8. She is sure that the presents are
for you. 9. The newspapers belong to us, but the book
belongs to you. 10. Where is the poor old woman? Is she
here? No. She is in the town with the farmer.

Have a Try 3

A la porte d'un palais à Paris trois officiers descendent
d'une voiture. La grande maison est à une personne très
importante, le Président de la République. Les soldats qui
sont devant l'entrée principale sont dans l'uniforme de la
garde républicaine. Les trois visiteurs sont très distingués:
le premier est un général, le second est un amiral et le
troisième est un général de l'armée de l'air. Dans les batailles

avec les ennemis de la France ils ont été (*been*) très courageux
et ils sont invités à la maison présidentielle pour recevoir (*to
receive*) les médailles qui sont la récompense (*reward*) d'un
courage exceptionnel.

LESSON FOUR

HOW TO SAY (FOR INSTANCE) "I HAVE FOUND"

In almost any string of words we use one is likely to tell us who does something and another to tell us what he does. In "I speak" or "I work" the words "speak" and "work" show what I am doing. Words which describe an action or what happens to somebody are called verbs. So "to speak", "to give", "to arrive" are all verbs because they are used to show somebody doing something or something happening.

Now the French for "to give" is *donner*, but it doesn't tell us who is giving or when he is doing it: it simply means "to give". In *donner* the *donn-* conveys the general idea of giving and the *-er* corresponds to the "to" in the English "to give".

But suppose we want to say "I have given". "I have", as we know from the last lesson, is *j'ai*, but it's no use putting *donner* after it, because *donner* means only "to give", which is not what we want. What we need is the French for "given". To get it, all we have to do is to take away the *-er* from *donner* and put *-é* instead: *donné*. In fact, it will sound much the same as before, because *-er* and *-é* when tacked on to the main part or stem of a verb both sound very much like the "a" in "hay" or "May". Now there are hundreds of verbs in French ending in *-er*. For example, *trouver* is "to find". So to put into French "I have found the money", we begin with *j'ai*, replace the *-er* of *trouver* by *-é*, which gives us *trouvé*, and add *l'argent—J'ai trouvé l'argent*.

In the same way, we can ask a question. "Have you?", as we know, is *Avez-vous?*, so we can say to somebody: *Avez-vous trouvé la vache qui est dans le parc?* Have you found the cow which is in the park?

At this point, there are two rather "grammar-bookish" words that we must learn. When a verb has "to" in front of it, it is said to be in the "Infinitive". Secondly, the part of the verb that we use after "I have" is called the "Past Participle". We already know two Infinitives—*donner*, to give, and *trouver*, to find. Replacing the *-er* by *-é*, we have their Past Participles, and we can use the Past Participles of hundreds of other verbs in the same way. Here are a few examples:

Infinitive	*Past Participle*
acheter, to buy	*acheté*, bought
marcher, to walk, to march	*marché*, walked, marched
voyager, to travel	*voyagé*, travelled
voler, to steal	*volé*, stolen
parler, to speak	*parlé*, spoken
travailler, to work	*travaillé*, worked
cacher, to hide	*caché*, hidden
manger, to eat	*mangé*, eaten
regarder, to look at[1]	*regardé*, looked at
chercher, to look for[1]	*cherché*, looked for

Word List 4

le tableau, the picture	*la viande*, the meat
le jour, the day	*hier*, yesterday
le propriétaire, the landlord, owner	*parce que*, because
le chien, the dog	*pour*, in order to
les vacances, the holidays (*fem. pl.*)	*passer*, to spend (of time)
	fâché, cross, angry

Exercise 4 (*a*)

Put into English:

1. Nous avons passé deux jours à Paris avec un ami. 2. La fermière est très fâchée parce que le méchant petit garçon a volé la viande. 3. Une vieille actrice a acheté la belle maison où nous avons passé les vacances. 4. Nous avons parlé à l'homme qui a acheté les chevaux. 5. Ils ont voyagé à la ville pour chercher un ami. 6. Avez-vous trouvé les journaux? Non. Mais je suis sûr qu'ils sont ici. 7. Les

[1] *regarder* means "to look *at*" and *chercher* means "to seek" or "to look *for*", so neither *à* nor *pour* is needed.

hommes qui ont travaillé hier dans les champs sont dans les
bois. 8. Les soldats ont marché à la ville. 9. Un méchant
homme a volé l'argent de la pauvre femme. 10. La petite
fille à qui j'ai parlé hier a passé les vacances à Londres.

Exercise 4 (b)

Put into French:

1. Where have you hidden the money? Behind a tree in
the garden. 2. They have bought a boat in order to spend
the holidays with a friend. 3. We have travelled to Paris in
order to look at the shops. 4. Have you looked for the poor
old dog? 5. Yes. He is with two other dogs in the field
behind the church. 6. I have spoken to the man who has
bought the hotel. 7. We are sure that she has spent three
days in (at) Paris. 8. They have looked in the house and in
the garden, but have they found the money? 9. Have you
bought the newspaper? No, but we have bought two books.
10. Yesterday we (have) walked to the town to buy a present
for a friend.

Have a Try 4

Le Prince de X, qui est le propriétaire d'un grand château en Italie, a une très belle collection de tableaux, de livres rares et d'autres objets précieux. Hier un criminel, armé d'un revolver, a pénétré dans la grande galerie de la vaste maison avec l'intention de voler un diamant d'une valeur énorme. Mais un chien fidèle (*faithful*) a donné l'alarme, un domestique a téléphoné à la police et deux agents (de police) ont arrêté le bandit.

LESSON FIVE

HOW TO SAY "OF THE" AND "TO THE"

In the first Word List we saw that *de* = "of" or "from" and that *à* = "to" or "at". In that same Lesson we saw that "the" is either *le, la, l'* or *les*, according to the noun it goes with. Therefore, clearly, "of the town " = *de la ville*; "from the hotel" = *de l'hôtel*; "to the church" = *à l'église*; and *à la mère* = to the mother.

We should expect therefore that "of the boy" would be *de le garçon* and that "to the garden" would be *à le jardin*.

Yet both would be wrong!

"Of the" before a masculine noun (except one beginning with a vowel or "mute" "h") is *du* NOT *de le*.

"To the" in the same way is *au* NOT *à le*.

"Of the" before any plural noun is *des* NOT *de les* and "to the" before any plural noun is *aux* NOT *à les*.

So we have, for instance:

du garçon, of the boy; *des garçons*, of the boys
de l'arbre, of the tree; *des arbres*, of the trees
à l'homme, to the man; *aux hommes*, to the men
au magasin, to (at) the shop; *aux magasins*. to (at) the shops

In English, we can say, for instance, "the doctor's house" or "John's hat". In French we can't do this. We must say instead "the house of the doctor", *la maison du médecin*, and "the hat of John", *le chapeau de Jean*.

How to Say "not" in French

The French for "not" is made up of two short words *ne* and *pas*. "I am", as we know, is *je suis*. The French for "I am not" is *je ne suis pas*. From this we can make a general rule. Put *ne* before the verb (*suis, avons* or whatever it happens to be) and *pas* immediately after it.

nous sommes, we are; *nous ne sommes pas*, we are not (we aren't)

17

Just as *le* is shortened into *l'* or *je* into *j'* before a vowel, so *ne* becomes *n'*.

J'ai, I have; *je n'ai pas,* I have not (I haven't)
I have found, *j'ai trouvé*

In the same way:

elle est, elle n'est pas, she is (not)
vous avez, vous n'avez pas, you have (not)
le chien de Jean n'est pas dans le jardin, John's dog isn't in the garden

When we want to say "I have not found" we put the *ne* before the *ai* and the *pas* immediately after it (so that the *pas* comes BEFORE the participle *trouvé*).

So:

je n'ai pas trouvé, I have not found
nous n'avons pas acheté le journal, we haven't bought the newspaper

Word List 5

près de, near, near to	*le visiteur,* the visitor
pendant que, while	*la bottine,* the boot
aujourd'hui, today	*le médecin,* the doctor
le marché, market	*le touriste,* the tourist
partout, everywhere	*intéressant,* interesting
malade, ill	*sans,* without
la fenêtre, window	*visiter,* to visit
pourquoi?, why?	*une heure,* hour
le pays, country, district	

Exercise 5 (*a*)

Put into English:

1. J'ai parlé hier au propriétaire du château. 2. L'eau du fleuve n'est pas très profonde. 3. Nous avons passé deux heures au jardin, pendant que les autres touristes ont visité l'église près du marché. 4. Avez-vous acheté le journal d'aujourd'hui? Non, les journaux ne sont pas très intéressants. 5. La mère de Jean est très fâchée parce que le méchant petit garçon a volé le chapeau du médecin. 6. Nous avons cherché partout les petits fils du fermier. 7. Sont-ils malades? Non, je suis sûr qu'ils ne sont pas malades. 8. Où

avez-vous caché les deux livres qui sont au cousin de Jean?
Je n'ai pas caché les livres: ils sont sur la table près de la
fenêtre. 9. Pourquoi avez-vous cherché hier les touristes?
Ils ne sont pas ici, je suis sûr qu'ils sont à Paris. 10. Au
petit magasin près du marché nous avons acheté trois livres
pour la cousine de Jean.

Exercise 5 (*b*)

Put into French:

1. We have spoken of you to the landlord of the hotel
which is near the market. 2. The dog which is in the field
does not belong to us, but to the farmer. 3. The officer and

the soldiers have marched from the town to the king's
palace. 4. The tourists have spent three days at Tours in
order to visit the old castles of the district. 5. We have looked
everywhere for the landlord's dog. 6. The actress who is at
the hotel is very angry because the dog has hidden two old
boots in the bed. 7. The officer's wife has bought a nice
little house. 8. It[1] is not near the town, but it is near the

[1] Refers to "the house".

river. 9. We have not visited the church, but we have looked
at the pictures in the king's palace. 10. I have spoken to the
doctor's young sons.

Have a Try 5

Dans un livre très célèbre un auteur a raconté les aven-
tures d'un petit garçon qui a trouvé dans les bagages d'un
vieux marin (*sailor*) la carte (*map*) d'une île où un pirate a
caché un vaste trésor. Un homme très riche à qui le garçon a
parlé de la carte a décidé de (*to*) voyager à la recherche (*in
search of*) du trésor. Le voyage n'est pas sans incident parce
que les marins qui ont accompagné l'homme et le garçon
sont en réalité les anciens camarades du pirate.

LESSON SIX

HOW TO USE WORDS OF NATIONALITY AND COLOUR

We have already used words such as *bon* and *long*—*un bon livre, une longue rue*—and we know that these words which tell us something about the noun they go with are called adjectives. In English such words come in front of their noun. In French they sometimes come after it. How are we to know which to do?

The general rule is that when the adjective is short and one that we use often it goes before the noun.

un grand palais, a great palace   *une petite ville*, a little town

But if the word is one of nationality or colour it comes after the noun.

un soldat français, a French   *une actrice américaine*, an
soldier   American actress
un chapeau gris, a grey hat

Notice, by the way, that adjectives of nationality in French are written with a small not a capital letter. *Un Français* would mean "a Frenchman".

Adjectives that are long or not very often used also come after their nouns.

un livre intéressant, an interesting   *un homme courageux*, a brave
book   man

How to Say "My", "His" or "Your"

So far we have been using only "the" or "a" with nouns. But if we want to say "your hat", not just "a hat", or "his aunt" instead of "an aunt", how is it to be done? Here below is the full list of all the words we may need to use:

Masc. Sing.		Fem. Sing.	Plural
My	*mon*	*ma*	*mes*
(thy)	*(ton)*	*(ta)*	*(tes)*
his (her)	*son*	*sa*	*ses*
our	*notre*	*notre*	*nos*
your	*votre*	*votre*	*vos*
their	*leur*	*leur*	*leurs*

There's no need to be scared of this list. It simply means that if the noun is masculine we use one of the words in the first column: *le chapeau* is "the hat", so "my hat" is *mon chapeau*. If the noun is feminine we use a word from the second column: *la maison* is "the house", so "my house" is *ma maison*. With any plural nouns we use a word from the third column: so *mes chapeaux* and *mes maisons*.

BUT there is one very important point to remember. In English we say "his book" if the book belongs to a boy and "her book" if it belongs to a girl. In other words, we go by the sex of the person the thing belongs to. Now, in French, as we know, "the" is *le* if its noun is masculine and *la* if its noun is feminine. It is the same with "my", "his" and the rest. Suppose we want to say "her aunt". *Tante* is feminine, so the possessive words (that is the "my", "his", etc.) must be feminine too. So we put *sa tante*. But what about "his aunt"? We can't put *son tante*, because *tante* is feminine. Therefore we must put *sa tante* here also. So *sa tante* means either "his aunt" or "her aunt", and *son père* means either "his father" or "her father".

So the rule is: Go by the gender of the noun and NOT by the sex of the owner.

Examples:

son oncle, his (her) uncle   *sa mère,* his (her) mother
ma sœur, my sister   *mon frère,* my brother
sa vache, his (her) cow   *son cheval,* his (her) horse
Le roi est dans son château. The king is in his castle.
La reine n'est pas dans son palais. The queen is not in her palace.
Ma cousine n'a pas trouvé ses journaux. My cousin has not found her
   newspapers.
L'officier et ses hommes. The officer and his men.

Tu = thou, and we shall very seldom use it. Therefore we shall not need *ton* (thy), but use *votre* for "your" just as we use *vous* for "you".

Word List 6

We saw in Lesson 4 that the Past Participle of many verbs ends, like *donné*, in *é*. There are some, however, which are irregular. Here are a few of them:

pris, taken
fait, done *or* made
le kilomètre, kilometre (⅝ of a mile)
le train, train
la semaine, week
le village, village
mis, put

vu, seen
le père, father
une excursion, excursion
noir, black
blanc (blanche), white
anglais, English

Exercise 6 (*a*)

Put into English:

1. Mes cousines et l'actrice américaine ont pris le train pour Bordeaux. 2. Nos amis français ont acheté une jolie maison blanche à deux kilomètres de la ville où nous avons passé nos vacances. 3. Avez-vous fait un voyage intéressant avec votre père? 4. Oui. Nous avons passé trois semaines

dans un petit village près du Mont Blanc. 5. Le touriste qui est le propriétaire de la grande voiture noire est anglais mais sa femme est française. 6. Mes deux amis italiens et leur petite sœur ont fait hier une belle excursion. 7. Qui a mis la vieille vache noire dans ma belle voiture? 8. Avez-vous vu ma fille? Elle n'est pas à l'école. 9. Mes fils et leurs amis sont dans un des petits bateaux qui sont au médecin de notre village. 10. Ma tante a les cheveux gris, mais elle n'est pas vieille.

Exercise 6 (*b*)

Put into French:

1. Where have you put my French newspapers? They are not on the table in my room. 2. Our doctor and his old mother have taken the train for Paris. 3. Your sisters are not here. They are in a boat on the river with two young men

from the village. 4. The old grey churches in our villages are interesting, but are they beautiful? 5. Our doctor and his aunt have spent their holidays in Paris. 6. My sister and her son have visited the old palaces of the French kings. 7. The farmer's wife is very angry because your sheep are in her garden. 8. The black boots do not belong to you. 9. We have looked at the white house where you have spent your holidays. 10. We have worked today with the farmer's two sons in the woods behind their house.

Have a Try 6

Les rues au centre de Paris sont, en général, très larges (*wide*) mais quand j'ai fait ma première (*first*) visite à Paris avec deux amis d'école, nous avons trouvé une certaine difficulté à traverser les rues à cause du grand nombre de voitures, de taxis et d'autobus qui ont passé et parce que le code de la route est différent en France où il est nécessaire de (*to*) tenir (*keep to*) la droite.

Dans un magasin près de notre hôtel j'ai acheté un plan de Paris et nous avons visité les principaux monuments (*public buildings*) de la ville, par exemple, le Louvre, un ancien palais royal qui est aujourd'hui un musée, et la cathédrale de Notre Dame.

LESSON SEVEN

MAINLY REVISION

At this point it will be helpful to add a little to what we have learned so far without tackling anything quite new.

1. More about "the"

In English we sometimes leave "the" out. In French we must put in *le* unless there is some very good reason for not doing so.

the king and queen, *le roi et la reine*
Money is useful, *l'argent est utile*

But in French as in English we do not need "the" (*le*, etc.) before the names of towns or cities.

Londres est une grande ville. London is a big city.
Il est à Paris. He is in Paris.

2. More about Asking Questions

(*a*) We know that we can turn, for instance, *il est* or *vous êtes* into questions by changing them over and linking the second word to the first by a "dash" *est-il?*, is he?; *êtes-vous?*, are you?

With *il a* (he has) we should expect to put *a-il?* But to avoid the awkward sound of two vowels "a" and "i" coming together, the French put a "-t-" in the middle and say *a-t-il?* or *a-t-elle?*: has he (she)? In fact, this happens only when the first word (the verb) ends in an "a" (as here) or in an "e".

(*b*) *To ask a question with "not" in it: il est*, he is; *il n'est pas*, he is not (he isn't), is he?, *est-il?* So to make it into "isn't he?" all we need do is to move *il* to the other side of *est*, linking it by a dash so that the *ne* (*n'*) is the first word and the *pas* the last: *n'est-il pas?*

26

Again, *nous sommes*; *nous ne sommes pas*; *sommes-nous?*; *ne sommes-nous pas?* are we not (aren't we?)?

And yet again: *vous avez trouvé*, you have found; *vous n'avez pas trouvé*. Reverse the order of *vous* and *avez* and we have *n'avez-vous pas trouvé?* have you not found?

3. How to Say "I found"

If you are asked whether you have seen someone you might say in reply: "Yes. I have just seen him." But you might quite well say instead: "Yes, I saw him just now." Both mean exactly the same thing. So, while the words *j'ai* and *trouvé* put together as *j'ai trouvé* mean, as we know, "I have found", they can also mean "I found". In the same way, *j'ai parlé* can mean "I have spoken" or "I spoke".

In the same way in questions: *avez-vous vu?* can mean either "have you seen?" or "did you see?".

But remember that you must not leave the *ai* out in French, even though it's not there in English. "The dog stole the meat" or "the dog has stolen the meat"—*Le chien a volé la viande.*

Word List 7

plus, more	*la campagne*, country (as opposed to town)
le monde, the world	*la place*, the square
la fleur, flower	*le travail*, work
un animal, animal	*tout* (masc.) *tous* (masc. pl.), all
intelligent, intelligent	*toute* (fem.), *toutes* (fem. pl.), all

Exercise 7 (a)

Put into English:

1. Les fleurs sont belles, les arbres sont utiles. 2. Les fils et les filles du médecin ont fait une excursion à la campagne. 3. Pourquoi n'avez-vous pas fait votre travail? 4. Où est votre sœur? A-t-elle pris le train pour Bordeaux avec ses amies? 5. Qui sont les petites filles à qui vous avez parlé au marché? 6. Elles sont les cousines de l'homme qui a acheté

la grande maison blanche près de l'église. 7. Le père et la
mère de Marie sont les propriétaires d'un petit magasin dans
la place du marché. 8. Pourquoi n'a-t-elle pas pris tous ses
livres à l'école? 9. Les éléphants sont plus intelligents que

les moutons. 10. Un des officiers a acheté toutes les vaches
blanches qui sont dans le champ du fermier.

Exercise 7 (b)

Put into French:

1. My father and mother have travelled in all the countries
of the world. 2. The dog is an animal which is very useful to
men. 3. All animals are not intelligent. 4. Why has he not
taken the money which is on the table in his room?
5. Where did you buy the old books? I bought all the books
in a little shop behind the church. 6. I did not see my
friend's (*masc.*) aunt, because we spent all the week in the
country. 7. The old Italian actress has bought the grey car
for her sons and daughters. 8. Where has she hidden her
money? 9. All the soldiers marched (walked) behind their
officer to the palace. 10. Have you looked for your books
in all the rooms in (of) the house?

Have a Try 7

Dans un journal parisien j'ai trouvé hier une histoire très amusante. Mme[1] X est employée comme (*as*) secrétaire dans un grand magasin près de la Seine. Elle n'est pas riche mais elle a la passion des (*for*) fleurs. Elle a l'habitude (*habit*) de poser (*place*) un vase de fleurs sur le rebord (*ledge*) du balcon. Hier par erreur elle a laissé (*let*) tomber (*fall*) son vase juste au moment où le propriétaire de la maison, un homme de très méchante humeur, est sur le point d'entrer

dans le magasin. Le pauvre homme est à l'hôpital et Mme X est obligée de (*to*) chercher une autre situation.

[1] *Mme = Madame* = Mrs.

LESSON EIGHT

HOW TO SAY "I GIVE"

In Lesson Four we saw that there are in French hundreds of verbs such as *trouver* (to find) and *donner* (to give) which end in *-er*, the *donn-* and the *trouv-* being the stem or root and the *-er* corresponding to the "to" in "to give" or "to find". By removing the *-er* and putting *é* instead we got *donné* (given) and *trouvé* (found) and we were able to put *j'ai* in front of it to give us "I have found" or (see Lesson Seven) "I found". Now, "I found" refers to something that is over, something that has already happened in the past. In this lesson we want to be able to describe something that is going on now, in the present. We want what is called the Present Tense—"I find" or "I give".

To get this all we need to do is to take the verb, knock off the *-er* and put these six endings instead: *-e, -es, -e, -ons, -ez, -ent*. So we have:

Present Tense

je donne, I give	*nous donnons*, we give
tu donnes, thou givest	*vous donnez*, you give
il (elle) donne, he (she) gives	*ils (elles) donnent*, they give

NOTE that *-e, -es* and *-ent* when tacked on to the stem (*donn-*) in this way are not pronounced at all, so that four out of the six sound alike, but the *je, il, ils* make the meaning clear. The *-ez* has much the same "a" sound as the *-er* of *donner* or the *-é* in *donné*.

"I give" is not the only meaning of *je donne*. In English we can say, for instance, "you speak". But if we change this into a question we cannot say "speak you?". We have to say either "do you speak?" or, more probably, "are you speaking?". In other words, *je donne* can mean not just "I give" but also "I do give" or "I am giving", because all three describe something going on now, in the present. So,

30

if we want to say "he is crossing the road" we put *il traverse la rue* and we do not (repeat NOT!) drag in *il est* just because the words "he is" are there in the English.

In the same way in "Are you going to the pictures?" there is no *êtes-vous*, but simply *allez-vous* (from *aller*, to go) *au cinéma?*. "You go", "you do go" or "you are going" = *vous allez:* they are all "in the present" and are merely slightly different ways in English of saying the same thing.

How to Say "this" and "that"

So far we know how to say "the book" or "my book". Now we come to "this book" or "that man". This is how it is done:

"This" or "that" before any masculine singular noun (except one beginning with a vowel or mute "h") is *ce*.

ce cheval, this (that) horse

"This" or "that" before any masculine singular noun beginning with a vowel or mute "h" is *cet*.

cet arbre, this (that) tree   *cet hôtel*, this (that) hotel

The *t* in *cet* is there only to avoid the awkward sound of two vowels coming together, as would happen without it. *Ce arbre* would sound ugly, but with *cet arbre* the words run smoothly. But the *t* is only there for the sound, so if we put in a word which doesn't begin with a vowel, then we can use the ordinary *ce*.

cet arbre; but *ce grand arbre*

"This" or "that" before any feminine singular noun is *cette*.

cette vache, this (that) cow   *cette église*, this (that) church

"This" or "that" before any plural noun is *ces*.

ces voitures, these (those) cars   *ces hommes*, these (those) men

There is therefore no difference between the French for "this" and the French for "that". But if we need to distinguish between the two we do it by tacking on -*ci* (short for *ici*—here) or *là*, which means "there". This man is my father, that man is my uncle: *cet homme-ci est mon père, cet homme-là est mon oncle.*

Word List 8

monter, to mount, to get into
demeurer, to live, dwell
traverser, to cross
tomber, to fall
dur, hard
le repas, meal

vilain, ugly
souvent, often
la vie, life, living
longtemps, (for) a long time
une usine, a factory
vers, towards

Exercise 8 (*a*)

Put into English:

1. Dans cet hôtel les repas sont très bons. 2. Les deux hommes qui montent dans cette voiture-là sont les frères de votre ami Jean. 3. Où avez-vous acheté ces cadeaux? 4. Qui demeure dans cette vilaine petite maison? 5. Où allez-vous? Nous allons visiter ce grand château à trois kilomètres du village. 6. Cette petite fille-là n'est pas très intelligente. Quand elle traverse le fleuve elle tombe souvent dans l'eau. 7. Pourquoi regardez-vous cette vieille femme? Qui est-elle? 8. Avez-vous demeuré longtemps dans cette ville? 9. Pour ces femmes-là qui travaillent dans une usine la vie est souvent très dure. 10. Nous sommes sûrs que ce garçon qui monte dans ce train-là est le fils du fermier.

Exercise 8 (*b*)

Put into French:

1. Who is that young man who is walking towards the church? 2. Do you live in one of those old houses which belong to our doctor? 3. Do you not go often to the cinema with your mother and father? 4. We live in the town but my aunt has spent her life in the country. 5. We often[1] go to the

[1] Put "often" after "go" in French.

factory in my father's car, but yesterday we took the train.
6. All the sheep which are crossing the road belong to that
farmer who bought your house. 7. Where have you put
your money? I hide my money while I am at school.
8. We are going to give the meat, which is on that table, to
the dog. 9. My brother works in a factory (at) three
kilometres from the town. 10. Do you go often to Rome?
I have lived for a long time in (*à*) Rome, and I have visited
all the big Italian towns.

Have a Try 8

Les touristes montent dans l'autobus et après (*after*) une
heure ils arrivent à l'entrée de l'aéroport de Londres. Là
l'autobus descend dans un long passage qui ressemble à un
tunnel et remonte à la surface. Une jolie fille qui est une
employée de la Compagnie "Air-France" guide les voyageurs au point de départ. Ils montent dans l'intérieur du
grand avion. Le pilote, le navigateur et le radio ont pris
déjà (*already*) leurs places. Les grands moteurs à réaction
(*jet*) sont mis en marche et le voyage aérien commence.

LESSON NINE

HOW TO SAY "HIM" OR "THEM"

In a sentence such as, for instance, "The train arrives" we know that "arrives" is the verb, because it tells us that something is going on or being done. "The train" is what we call the "subject", that is the person or thing that does whatever is the action or event that the verb describes. "The train arrives", consisting of subject and verb, is about as short a sentence as we can get. But if we have instead, say, "The hunter kills" the sentence is not complete, it doesn't make proper sense until we know what the man kills: we have to complete it by adding, for example, "the tiger": *Le chasseur tue le tigre.* In this sentence *le chasseur* is the subject, *tue* is the verb, and *le tigre* is known as the object of the verb. It's not difficult to find the object of a verb. In, for instance, "the boy eats the apples" "eats" is the verb. If we ask "who eats?" the answer is "the boy", and that is the subject. If we then say "eats what?" the answer is "the apples", and that is what grammar-books call "the object" of the verb: *Le garçon mange les pommes.* In "the tiger eats the boy", on the other hand, "the tiger" is clearly the subject, and when we ask "eats whom?" this time "the boy" being "the eaten", not "the eater", is the object: *Le tigre mange le garçon.* As with nouns, so with pronouns. If we say "he eats them" we know that "he eats" is *il mange* (subject and verb) and "them" is the object. *Ils* is "they", but what are we to put for "them" (object)? The list below will show you.

Subject Pronoun		Object Pronoun	
French	*English*	*French*	*English*
je	I	*me*	me
(tu)	(thou)	*(te)*	(thee)
il	he (*or* it, *masc.*)	*le*	him (*or* it, *masc.*)
elle	she (*or* it, *fem.*)	*la*	her (*or* it, *fem.*)
nous	we	*nous*	us
vous	you	*vous*	you
ils	they (*masc.*)	*les*	them (*masc.*)
elles	they (*fem.*)	*les*	them (*fem.*)

It's easy to remember these: *me* has the same spelling in French and in English, *nous* and *vous* are the same, whether as subject or object, *te* we shall hardly ever use, while *le*, *la* and *les* are the same to look at as the French for "the".

But there is one very important rule. When the object of a verb is a noun it usually comes AFTER the verb, but when the object of a verb is a pronoun it usually comes BEFORE the verb. So:

il mange les pommes, BUT *il les mange*, he eats them

Here are some further examples:

(Où est votre argent?) Je l'ai ici. I have it here.
Je la cherche. I am looking for her.
Elle nous regarde. She is looking at us.
Nous les regardons. We are looking at them.
Votre ami vous cherche. Your friend is looking for you.
Nous l'achetons. We buy it.

REMEMBER that the object pronoun comes immediately in front of the verb, so if there is a "not" in the sentence the *ne* gets pushed to the left to make room for the object pronoun. So:

je ne cherche pas le garçon, BUT *je ne le cherche, pas,* I am not looking for him

AGAIN, when the verb is made up of, say, *j'ai* + a past participle the object pronoun must come in front of the whole verb, not merely in front of the past participle.

j'ai trouvé mon journal   *je l'ai trouvé*

In a question the same is true:

Avez-vous trouvé mon journal?
L'avez-vous trouvé?
N'avez-vous pas trouvé mon journal?
Ne l'avez-vous pas trouvé? Haven't you found it?

Now for Some Practice

Word List 9

le cahier, exercise- (note-) book	*quelquechose*, something
le billet, ticket	*une heure*, hour, o'clock
perdu, lost	*après*, after, afterwards
un avion, an aeroplane	*toujours*, always
un autobus, a (motor) bus	

Exercise 9 (*a*)

Put into English:

1. Cherchez-vous quelquechose? Oui. Je cherche mes livres, mais je ne les trouve pas. 2. Où avez-vous mis votre cahier? Je l'ai mis sur la table dans ma chambre. 3. Où est mon chien? L'avez-vous vu? Non, je ne l'ai pas vu. 4. Où allez-vous passer vos vacances? Nous les passons toujours à

la campagne. 5. Pourquoi n'avez-vous pas pris le train?
Je ne l'ai pas pris parce que je n'ai pas mon billet. 6. L'avez-
vous perdu? Non. Votre méchant petit chien l'a mangé.
7. J'ai cherché partout le médecin, mais je ne l'ai pas
trouvé. 8. Qui est cet homme-là qui nous regarde? 9. Votre
sœur n'est pas à l'école. N'a-t-elle pas fait son travail?
10. Oui, elle l'a fait, mais elle est à la maison aujourd'hui
parce qu'elle est malade.

Exercise 9 (*b*)

Put into French:

1. That hat is not pretty. Where did you buy it? 2. I did
not buy it. I found it in the bus. 3. I am looking for my
brother. Haven't you seen him? 4. No, I haven't seen him,
but I am sure that he is not here. 5. Are you looking for her?
No. I am not looking for her. 6. Where do you buy your
exercise-books? We buy them at the little shop near the
church. 7. My brother's books are not in his room. Where
does he hide[1] them? 8. Your sister's present is not here.
Where has she hidden it? 9. Where is your brother? Is he
ill? No. I saw him yesterday. 10. Where are the tickets?
Have you (got) them? Yes. I have them.

Have a Try 9

Charles a fait le voyage de Londres à Paris par avion. Il
passe une semaine de ses vacances en France avec Jean, un
ami français, qui demeure avec son père et sa mère dans une
jolie petite maison près du Bois de Boulogne. Hier Charles
a fait avec Jean une longue promenade par les rues de Paris.
Après deux heures de marche ils ont cherché un café, et
Charles, qui est fatigué, est très content de manger une bonne
glace à la vanille pendant qu'il observe les taxis et les
voitures qui passent sous (*under*) le regard attentif d'un
agent de police, son bâton blanc à la main (*hand*).

[1] Would *cache-il* sound right?

LESSON TEN

HOW TO SAY "SOME" OR "ANY"

So far we know how to put into French "the apple", "my apple", "this apple", but we do not yet know how to put into French "some butter", "any money" or "some apples". In fact, we have not got to learn anything new in order to be able to do this, because the various ways of saying "of the" will also serve to mean "some" or "any".

So, before any singular noun beginning with a vowel or mute "h", "some" or "any" is *de l'*:

> *de l'argent* (masc.), some (any)   *de l'eau* (fem.), some (any) water
> money

BEFORE any masculine singular noun (except one beginning with a vowel or mute "h") "some" or "any" is *du*:

> *du pain*, some (any) bread   *du vin*, some (any) wine

BEFORE any feminine singular noun (except one beginning with a vowel or mute "h") "some" or "any" is *de la*:

> *de la viande*, some (any) meat   *de la bière*, some (any) beer

BEFORE any plural noun "some" or "any" is *des*:

> *des crayons* (masc.), pencils   *des valises* (fem.), some suitcases
> *un(e) enfant*, a child   *des enfants*, some (any) children

How to Say "there is" or "there are"

These are words we want to use very often. The French for them is *il y a*. "There is" or "there are" are BOTH in French *il y a*.

There is a chair near the window. *Il y a une chaise près de la fenêtre.*
There are two birds in the cage. *Il y a deux oiseaux dans la cage.*

How to Say "whom" or "which"

Look at the middle bit of these two sentences:

(i) The man, *who saw your cousin*, is here.
(ii) The man, *whom you saw*, is my cousin.

For (i) the French is obviously: *L'homme, qui a vu votre cousin, est ici*, because the subject of the verb "saw" is clearly *qui* and refers to *l'homme*. But in (ii) we find the subject of "saw" by asking "who saw"? and the answer is "you", so this time "whom" is not the subject but the object, and we translate it by *que*.

L'homme que vous avez vu est mon cousin.

In correct English the use of "who" or "whom" will tell us whether we should put *qui* or *que*, but there is no such guide when the English is "which", so we must be very careful to find out whether "which" is the subject or whether it is the object of the verb it comes in front of.

the bread which is on the table, *le pain qui est sur la table*
the bread which I have bought, *le pain que j'ai acheté*

Word List 10

sous, under	*parmi*, among
la main, hand	*le beurre*, butter
un agent de police, policeman	*par*, by, through
un voyageur, a traveller	*le déjeuner*, lunch
ou, or	*désirer*, to wish (to), to want (to)
le fromage, cheese	*le café*, coffee (*or* a café)

Exercise 10 (*a*)

Put into English:

1. Parmi les animaux dans le jardin zoologique il y a deux éléphants et des tigres. 2. Qui est cet enfant qui a un crayon à[1] la main? 3. Les crayons que vous avez à la main sont à mon frère. 4. Désirez-vous du vin ou de la bière? 5. Les vins français sont souvent très bons. 6. Nous avons acheté de la viande et du fromage italien pour notre déjeuner. 7. Les hommes que vous regardez sont des soldats américains. 8. Les jeunes filles à qui vous avez parlé hier, sont des actrices. 9. Les voyageurs qui montent dans cet

[1]*à* = "in" here.

autobus ont passé deux jours dans notre petite ville. 10. Ma tante est très fâchée parce que le fromage qu'elle a acheté n'est pas bon.

Exercise 10 (*b*)

Put into French:

1. There are some policemen in front of the king's palace. 2. We have found the little dog which you lost yesterday. 3. Do you want to buy some books? There is a shop near the church where we buy them when we have any money. 4. The children who are looking through the window of that house are not at school today because they are ill. 5. We are going to buy some cheese and some apples for (the) lunch. 6. The king and queen are arriving at the castle. 7. There are some books which are not very interesting. 8. The actress lost some money, but a policeman found it in a suitcase under a bed at the hotel. 9. The animals which are in the field are horses.[1] 10. The house (which) you are looking at belongs to the doctor.

Have a Try 10

Charles et Jean ont pris l'autobus pour aller à Versailles. Les deux garçons ont trouvé des places sur la plateforme à

---

[1] REMEMBER that words such as "the", "some" and "which", often left out in English, should be put in in French.

l'arrière (*at the back*) de l'autobus, d'où ils ont regardé avec
intérêt les rues animées de la ville. Après une heure de
voyage ils arrivent à leur destination et descendent de
l'autobus à l'entrée du château. "De qui est cette statue?"
demande Charles. Il indique de la main la grande statue
d'un homme monté à cheval. "C'est le roi Louis XIV. Il a
régné (1643–1715) plus longtemps que (*than*) la Reine
Victoria (1837–1901). Au commencement de son règne
il a demeuré à Paris—au Louvre, mais à ses ordres une
armée d'hommes ont travaillé pour transformer la modeste
maison de campagne qui a existé ici dans le vaste château
que nous allons visiter après le déjeuner. Il y a un restaurant
près du château où les repas sont bons et les prix raison-
nables."

LESSON ELEVEN

HOW TO SAY "SHUT THE DOOR", ETC.

When we use a verb to give a command the form of the verb we use for doing this is called the Imperative. We do not, in fact, have to learn anything new, for in most cases, in English as in French, all we need to do is to drop off the "you" or *vous* from the Present Tense.

> you shut the door, *vous fermez la porte*
> Shut the door! *Fermez la porte!*
> Don't shut the door! *Ne fermez pas la porte!*

By taking the 1st plural of a French Present Tense and dropping off the *nous* we can change, say, "we are going" into "let us go".

> *nous allons au cinéma*, we are going to the pictures
> *allons au cinéma*, let's go to the pictures
> *cherchons nos amis*, let us look for our friends

How to Say "The door is shut"

As we know already, a word such as "good" or any other adjective must "agree" with the noun to which it refers: *le bon chien; la viande est bonne.* Now, compare these two sentences:

The door is white.   The door is shut.

For the first we should put: *La porte est blanche* (because *la porte* is a feminine noun and "white" must agree with it). Surely, if we say "The door is shut" there is no real difference. *Fermé* is the Past Participle of *fermer*, to shut. But it is used here in exactly the same way as *blanche*. In other words, the Past Participle of a verb used with "is" or "are" (or for that matter any part of the verb "to be") must, in fact, agree with its noun, just as an adjective does. So, we have:

La porte est blanche and *La porte est fermée.*

BUT, of course, this does not apply when the Past Participle is used with "have" or "has", because in "we (have) shut the door" "shut" is a verb not an adjective at all. So in French a Past Participle used with any part of the verb "to be" agrees with the subject of the verb, but a Past Participle used with any part of "to have" doesn't agree with the subject, but remains unchanged.

Nous avons fait notre travail. We have done our work.
La maison est faite de briques rouges. The house is made of red brick(s).

Numbers

We know already a few numbers. Here is the complete list up to twenty.

un(e), one	*six*, six,	*onze*, eleven	*seize*, sixteen
deux, two	*sept*, seven	*douze*, twelve	*dix-sept*, seventeen
trois, three	*huit*, eight	*treize*, thirteen	*dix-huit*, eighteen
quatre, four	*neuf*, nine	*quatorze*, fourteen	*dix-neuf*, nineteen
cinq, five	*dix*, ten	*quinze*, fifteen	*vingt*, twenty

Word List 11

situé (Past Participle), situated
rouge, red
vert, green
assis, seated, sitting
la gare, (railway) station
la chaise, chair

si, if (also "so")
casser, to break
avant, before (of time)
devant, before, in front of (of place)
le voleur, thief

Exercise 11 (*a*)

Put into English:

1. La maison où j'ai passé les vacances est située à quinze kilomètres de Paris. 2. Ma tante a demeuré longtemps dans cette maison qui a une porte rouge et un joli jardin. 3. Ce petit garçon qui a mangé hier dix-sept pommes vertes n'est pas à l'école aujourd'hui, parce qu'il est malade. 4. Ne tombez pas dans l'eau: elle est très profonde. 5. Si vous désirez arriver à Versailles avant deux heures, montez dans

cet autobus-là. 6. La jeune fille que vous cherchez est
assise à une table du Café de la Gare. 7. Parmi les voyageurs
qui montent dans le train de trois heures pour Paris il y a
quinze soldats américains, douze touristes italiens et tous
les enfants du médecin. 8. Si vous allez au jardin zoologique,
achetez des pommes et du pain pour donner aux animaux.
9. Toutes les fenêtres de notre maison sont cassées. Je suis

sûr que votre petit fils l'a fait. 10. Où est il? Dans le jardin.
Regardez! Il a une brique à la main!

Exercise 11 (b)

Put into French:

1. Look at those two little girls who are sitting in that
boat. 2. Let us cross the street in order to get into that bus.
3. If you want to buy some red pencils, go to the little shop
near the Café. 4. Do not eat that apple; it is green. 5. In
our village there are some houses which are made of wood.
6. It is eleven o'clock, let us go to the station. 7. Look for
my cousin: she is sitting on a chair in the garden. 8. We
have some friends who are arriving from London at nine
o'clock. 9. All the doors of the church are shut. 10. There
are some policemen who are looking everywhere for the
money which the thief has hidden.

Have a Try 11

Charles et Jean ont passé une heure agréable assis à une
table sur la terrasse du café où ils ont pris leur déjeuner.
Ils sont très contents parce que le repas a été (*been*) excellent.
A deux heures ils entrent dans le château et commencent à
marcher par les grandes galeries où ils admirent des tableaux
de toutes sortes, faits par des artistes célèbres—des portraits
de personnages historiques, des scènes de bataille. Il y a
aussi des tables, des chaises et des sculptures qui datent de
l'âge du roi Louis XIV ou de ses successeurs. Après une
heure les deux garçons entrent dans le grand parc du palais,
où il y a de longues avenues, qui sont bordées d'arbres et de
statues..

Jean consulte sa montre (*watch*). "Allons acheter des
cartes-postales et aussi (*also*) des fruits pour manger
pendant (*during*) le voyage de retour."

LESSON TWELVE

MORE ABOUT PRONOUNS

In Lesson Nine we saw that when a pronoun such as "him" was the object of a verb, the French for it was *le* and we put it in front of the verb: *je le trouve, je l'ai trouvé* and so on.

Now, in a sentence such as "I give him some money" the direct object is in fact some money, because the sentence really means "I give some money to him". Here "money" is the object and "to him" is what we call the indirect object. Again, we may have a sentence such as "We are going with him". Here there is no "object" of the verb at all. In "I give some money" we find the object by asking "Give what?", and the answer is "some money". But if we ask "Go what?" it doesn't make sense. There is no object. There is simply "with him". Words like "with", "without", "for", "under", etc., are known as prepositions, and we want to know how we are to put "him" or "us" into French after a preposition.

In Lesson Nine we put down two lists, the first consisting of "I", "she", etc., the second of "me", "him", etc. They are set out again here. But two other lists are added. The first of these new ones shows how we are to put "to me", "to him", etc., used as indirect objects ("he shows his book *to me*"), while the second new list shows what form of a pronoun we are to use after a preposition such as "with" or "for".

Subject	Direct Object	Indirect Object	With Prepositions
je	me	*me*, to me	*moi*, (with) me
(*tu*)	(*te*)	(*te*), to thee	*toi*, (with) thee
il	le	*lui*, to him, to it	*lui*, (with) him
elle	la	*lui*, to her, to it	*elle*, (with) her
nous	nous	*nous*, to us	*nous*, (with) us
vous	vous	*vous*, to you	*vous*, (with) you
ils	les	*leur*, to them	*eux*, (with) them (*masc.*)
elles	les	*leur*, to them	*elles*, (with) them (*fem.*)

The first two lists we know all about already, and they are merely put in here so that they can be compared with the third and fourth. REMEMBER that when a pronoun is an indirect object (List 3) it comes BEFORE the verb just as those in List 2 do. The words in List 4 do NOT come before the verb, but follow the "with" or whatever the preposition may be. Look at these examples:

I have given the book (*object*) to the boy (*indirect object*). *J'ai donné le livre au garçon.*

I have given it (*object*) to the boy (*indirect object*). *Je l'ai donné au garçon.*

I have given him the book = I have given the book (*object*) to him (*indirect object*). *Je lui ai donné le livre.*

Il nous a donné un cadeau. He has given (to) us a present.

Let us go with him. *Allons avec lui.*

Let us go without her. *Allons sans elle.*

NOTE that *nous* and *vous* are the same in all four lists. The tricky one is *lui* (which in List 3 means either (to) him or (to) her, but used with, say, *avec, lui* means "(with) him" only: with her = *avec elle.*

One or two other examples:

Cette pomme est pour lui (for him).

Ces pommes sont pour eux (masc.), *pour elles* (fem.)—"for them".

Il m'a donné de l'argent: Vous a-t-il donné de l'argent? Did he give you some money?

Ne lui avez-vous pas donné ces livres? Didn't you give him these books? (these books to him?)

How to say "I shall find", etc.

If we write down the Present *j'ai* and so on, leaving out all the pronouns, we have *ai, as, a, avons, avez, ont.* Next, cut out the *av* from *avons* and *avez.* We then have *-ai, -as, -a, -ons, -ez* and *-ont.* Now take the Infinitive (the part of the verb which ends in *-er*): *trouver*, "to find", and add to it the six endings. We then have the Future Tense ("I shall find").

je trouverai, I shall find   *nous trouverons*, we shall find
(tu) trouveras, thou shalt find   *vous trouverez*, you will find
il (elle) trouvera, he (she) will find   *ils (elles) trouveront*, they will find

By adding these same six endings we can form the Future Tense of hundreds of other verbs: *je donnerai, je parlerai* and so on.

Word List 12

été (Past Participle), been
dit (Past Participle), said, told
écrit (Past Participle), written
pendant, during

pendant que, while
déjà, already
aussi, also
apporter, to bring

la montre, the watch
la lettre, the letter
porter, to carry
un franc, a franc (worth about 1*s*. 9*d*.)
envoyer, to send
une carte-postale, a postcard
le neveu, nephew
la nièce, niece

Exercise 12 (*a*)

Put into English:

1. Si ces deux enfants désirent aller au cinéma je leur donnerai quatre francs pour acheter les billets. 2. Mes frères et leurs amis ne sont pas ici, mais si vous allez à la gare je suis sûr que vous les trouverez. 3. Il y a une lettre pour vous sur la table. 4. Mon père m'a envoyé une carte-postale de Londres. 5. Hier je lui ai écrit une longue lettre. 6. Le cadeau que j'ai acheté est pour elle. 7. Les deux hommes à qui vous avez parlé hier ont été avec moi à l'école. 8. Il est déjà trois heures: allons au marché sans eux. 9. Le neveu et la nièce du médecin m'ont dit qu'il leur a donné vingt francs. 10. À qui sont ces deux montres? Cette montre-ci est à moi, mais l'autre est à lui.

Exercise 12 (*b*)

Put into French:

1. The old woman is very poor. If I have any money I will give her five francs. 2. If you give me two francs I will carry your suitcase. 3. Do not go to the hotel without him. 4. I have sent her a postcard. 5. Have you written to your

nephews? Yes. And we have sent them a present. 6. Our
dog is very intelligent. When I am sitting in the garden he

brings me my newspaper. 7. Where have you been? We
have been to the market with John and his sister. 8. Our
cousins are very angry because we do not want to go to the
pictures with them. 9. Have you seen the policeman? Yes.
I told him that a thief has taken my watch. 10. The boys are
not in the garden. Where shall we look for them?

Have a Try 12

Un jeune garçon, âgé de quinze ans, a fait une expédition
avec son père dans une région de l'Inde où il y a toutes
sortes de bêtes féroces. Un jour, pendant que son père est
absent du camp, ce garçon quitte sa tente et commence à
marcher par la forêt. Soudain il entend (*hears*) des cris
lamentables et trouve devant lui un éléphant qui a au pied
une longue épine (*thorn*). L'animal a un air si triste que le
garçon surmonte sa terreur. Il essaye de (*tries to*) retirer
l'épine et après deux ou trois efforts inutiles il accomplit
(*performs*) cette tâche (*task*) difficile et dangereuse.

Le temps passe et le garçon est maintenant (*now*) un père
de famille. Un jour il décide d'aller au cirque à Paris. Il

n'a pas une très bonne place parmi les spectateurs parce qu'il n'est pas riche.

Un éléphant entre dans l'arène (*ring*) et commence à faire (*do*) des tours (*tricks*). Soudain l'animal le remarque et le regarde fixement. Il s'approche de lui, le lève (*lifts*) dans l'air et le dépose sur une chaise au premier rang. L'éléphant a une bonne mémoire!

LESSON THIRTEEN

HOW TO SAY "MUCH", "MANY"

So far we know how to say, for instance, "some wine" or "some men". But how are we to say "much wine" or "many men" or, for that matter, "a glass of wine" or "a cup of tea"?

Think about these words for a minute. There is something that applies to all of them. They all indicate an amount of something. A glass, a cup or a bottle all indicate fairly fixed amounts, whereas "much (many)", "a crowd" are less exact, but they all have this same idea of amount or quantity. "A glass" and "a cup" are nouns, while words such as "much", "many", "enough" are what are called adverbs. That doesn't make any difference to the following rule:

When a noun or an adverb of amount or quantity is followed by another noun we put *de* before the second noun. We do this whether there is an "of" in the English or not.

> *une bouteille de vin*, a bottle of wine   *beaucoup de vin*, much wine

BUT, of course, *du vin*, "some wine" (because "a bottle" is a noun of quantity, but "some" is neither: it is simply our old friend "some" or "any").

For the same reason we do not need any *de* after ordinary numbers, such as *cinq* or *douze*.

> *cinq heures*, five hours (*or* five o'clock)   *douze hommes*, twelve men

BUT *une douzaine d'hommes*, a dozen men (*une douzaine* is a noun).

Word List 13

Adverbs of Quantity	Nouns of Quantity
peu, little, few	*une bouteille*, a bottle
beaucoup, much, many	*un verre*, a glass
tant, so much, so many	*une tasse*, a cup

51

trop, too much, too many   *une foule*, a crowd
combien, how much, how many?   *une douzaine*, a dozen
assez, enough, sufficient

le thé, tea   *maintenant*, now
le lait, milk   *le porteur*, (railway) porter
un œuf, an egg   *le compartiment*, (railway) com-
un gâteau, a cake   partment
le temps, time, weather   *prêter*, to lend
bu (Past Participle), drunk   *montrer*, to show
vendu (Past Participle), sold

Exercise 13 (*a*)

Put into English:

1. Il y a beaucoup d'hommes qui ont très peu d'argent.
2. Combien de vin français avez-vous acheté hier? 3. Nous avons acheté deux bouteilles de bon vin blanc et de la bière. 4. Il y a trop de voyageurs dans ce compartiment: montons dans un autre. 5. Si vous n'avez pas assez d'argent pour acheter le livre que vous désirez, je vous prêterai dix francs. 6. Cet homme qui monte dans le bateau a bu trop de vin. Je suis sûr qu'il tombera dans l'eau. 7. J'ai peu de fromage, mais j'ai un petit gâteau qui est très bon. 8. Le temps est si beau aujourd'hui que j'ai passé deux heures dans le jardin. 9. Nous avons passé très peu de temps à la campagne, mais nous avons fait trois excursions par autobus. 10. Ce petit garçon est malade aujourd'hui parce qu'il a mangé hier tant de gâteaux et de pommes.

Exercise 13 (*b*)

Put into French:

1. There are not enough porters at this station. 2. All the eggs are broken because your naughty nephew put them on the chair where his aunt is now sitting. 3. At the market we bought some tea and a dozen eggs. 4. There are a crowd of American tourists at the hotel. 5. How many suitcases have you? I am sure that the porter will bring them to the bus.

6. Why do you wish to get into a compartment where there are already a dozen travellers? 7. He has already drunk five cups of tea, and now he has bought a bottle of red wine. 8. I will show you the book which my friend has lent me. 9. We will not spend much time here because we want to visit the church. 10. We have not much money, but we will lend you two francs (in order) to buy cakes.

Have a Try 13

J'ai trouvé aujourd'hui dans un journal parisien un article au sujet d'un vol (*theft*) qui a été commis à Lyon. Un homme a téléphoné au propriétaire d'un grand cinéma et lui a dit que des voleurs ont l'intention d'entrer dans ce cinéma à une heure du matin (*morning*). Il assure le propriétaire qu'il a téléphoné à la police et que dans cinq minutes des agents de police arriveront au cinéma et qu'ils resteront (*remain*) cachés à l'intérieur pour arrêter les criminels au bon moment.

Cinq minutes après le propriétaire laisse entrer des hommes qui portent l'uniforme des agents de police. Leur chef (*chief*) invite le propriétaire à lui montrer le coffre-fort (*safe*) où il a mis l'argent que les spectateurs du programme lui ont payé pendant le jour. Le propriétaire ouvre (*opens*) le coffre-fort pour montrer que l'argent est intact (*untouched*). Les voleurs, déguisés en agents de police, forcent le propriétaire à leur donner le contenu du coffre-fort. Ils le laissent dans son bureau (*office*) les bras (*arms*) et les pieds attachés avec des cordes et ils sortent (*go out*) avec précaution dans la rue déserte.

LESSON FOURTEEN

MAINLY TIDYING UP

How to Say "Give me"

We know that we can give an order by, for instance, dropping the *vous* from *vous donnez*. We also know that when a pronoun is the direct or indirect object of a verb that pronoun in French comes in front of the verb.

> *Je le donnerai à votre mère* (Direct Object).
> *Il m'a donné un cadeau* (Indirect Object).

THERE IS one exception to this. When we give an order, using the Imperative (as it is called), the pronoun comes AFTER the verb, as in English

> Give it to your mother. *Donnez-le à votre mère.*
> Give him your ticket. *Donnez-lui votre billet.*

NOTE the - which links the object pronoun to the verb.

Now, we should expect "give me" to be *donnez-me*. But the French think this sounds ugly and, in this case only, they change *me* into *moi* and put *donnez-moi*. This putting the pronoun after the verb is done only when there is no "not" in the sentence. If there is a "not", then the object pronoun comes BEFORE the verb in the ordinary way.

> Show me your ticket. *Montrez-moi votre billet.*
> Don't show me your ticket. *Ne me montrez pas votre billet.*
> Let us give her that present. *Donnons-lui ce cadeau.*
> Don't let us give her this present. *Ne lui donnons pas ce cadeau.*
> I will show him my ticket. *Je lui montrerai mon billet.*
> I will not show him my ticket. *Je ne lui montrerai pas mon billet.*

These last two are only to remind you of what we learned in a previous lesson. Remember that it is only in the Imperative that the object pronoun ever comes after the verb, and then only if there is no "not".

Feminine of Adjectives

We know some rules already. Here is another.

If an adjective ends in -*x* it changes -*x* into -*se* to form the feminine.

heureux, (*masc.*) happy; *heureuse* (*fem.*), happy

Similarly,

malheureu-x(-se), unhappy; *courageu-x(-se)*, brave

How to Say "At (to) the baker's"

When we say "I am going to the baker's" or "I bought it at Wood's" we really mean "at the baker's" or "at Wood's shop". For this we use in French *chez*, a very useful word, which can mean "to (at) (in) the shop (house) of". So "to the baker's" is *chez le boulanger* and "at Wood's" might be *chez Dubois*. In the same way, if we ask "Is he in?" we really mean "Is he at home?" "Is he in his house?" and we put it as: *Est-il chez lui?* (at the house of him).

How to Say "Is there?"

Il a, of course, is "he has". Despite that, "there is" or "there are" is *il y a*.

Now, when we say "has he?" we have to put, not *a-il* but *a-t-il* to make it easier to say. So when we want to alter "there is" into "Is there" we must do the same:

Is there a doctor here? *Y a-t-il un médecin ici?*

Word List 14

le kilogramme, kilogramme (just over 2 lb. in weight)	*rencontrer*, to meet
le légume, the vegetable	*le boulanger*, baker
le matin, the morning	*le marchand*, shop-keeper, merchant
l'après-midi, the afternoon	*une chose*, a thing
la nuit, the night	*paresseux*, lazy
demain, tomorrow	*quelqu'un*, someone

Exercise 14 (a)

Put into English:

1. J'ai des choses à acheter au marché, mais je vous rencontrerai à trois heures chez Jean. 2. Il y a quelqu'un à la porte qui désire vous parler. 3. Vos valises sont très grandes: donnez-les au porteur. 4. Ces légumes ne sont pas bons: ne les achetez pas. 5. Qui est cet officier que nous avons rencontré hier chez votre tante? 6. Notre pauvre amie est très malheureuse, parce qu'elle a perdu tout son argent. 7. A qui avez-vous vendu votre vieille voiture? 8. Y a-t-il dans cette ville un bon hôtel? 9. J'ai acheté ce matin deux kilogrammes de pommes et six œufs. Je les apporterai chez vous cet après-midi. 10. Ces petites filles sont très paresseuses: quand elles sont à l'école elles ne travaillent pas.

Exercise 14 (d)

Put into French:

1. Is there any money on that table near the window? 2. Bring me the suitcase which you will find under my bed. 3. Our friends are now in Paris. Let us send (to) them a postcard. 4. There are some eggs on the table: do not break them. 5. This afternoon I bought three kilogrammes of butter at Dupont's. 6. I am looking for my uncle but someone told me that he is not at home. 7. Where will you meet us? I will meet you tomorrow at your brother's (house). 8. I saw your sister this morning. Why is she so unhappy? 9. During the night I saw someone in the garden behind the house of your friends: I am sure they are not at home. 10. If you have not lost your ticket, give it to the porter.

Have a Try 14

Hier vers onze heures de la nuit j'ai regardé par la fenêtre de ma chambre, parce que ma montre n'est pas très exacte et j'ai désiré savoir (*to know*) si elle est en avance en (*by*) la comparant avec l'horloge (*clock*) de l'église qui est près de chez moi. A ce moment j'ai remarqué avec surprise un homme qui est sur le point d'entrer par une fenêtre dans la maison de mon voisin, M. Leclerc. Sans hésitation j'ai téléphoné au poste de police pour signaler (*report*) cet incident. Bientôt (*soon*) des agents de police arrivent en voiture. Ils marchent avec précaution jusqu'à (*up to*) la porte de la maison de M. Leclerc. Quelqu'un l'ouvre (*opens*) et ils passent à l'intérieur.

Cinq minutes après ils quittent la maison et je suis surpris de remarquer que M. Leclerc est avec eux. Il est évident que j'ai fait une erreur. L'explication est simple. Quand M. Leclerc arrive chez lui il trouve qu'il a perdu sa clef (*key*). Sa femme passe deux jours à la campagne chez des amies et M. Leclerc que j'ai pris pour un voleur a été forcé d'entrer dans sa maison par une fenêtre.

LESSON FIFTEEN

ABOUT WORDS ENDING IN -ING

In an earlier lesson we saw that long adjectives are usually placed after the noun in French. One example given was *une histoire intéressante*, an interesting story. Now there is a verb *intéresser* just as we have the English verb "to interest" and the *-ant* in *intéressant* corresponds to the *-ing* in "interesting". This *-ant* tacked on to the stem *intéress-* gives us what we call the Present Participle—"interesting". Remember that the Past Participle would be *intéressé*—"interested". All Present Participles in French end in *-ant*: *portant*, *donnant*, just as in English they end in "-ing"—carrying, giving.

Now in *une histoire intéressante*, the "interesting" is simply an adjective, like "long" (story) or "short" (story), and therefore agrees with its noun.

BUT a Present Participle can be used as a Verb. In the sentence: "Going up the stairs, they arrive at their room" "going up" is clearly a verb and has in this example an object. (Going up what? Answer: the stairs.)

USED as an Adjective a Present Participle agrees with its noun. Used as a verb it does not alter

Montant (verb) *l'escalier ils arrivent à leur chambre.*
la marée montante (adjective), the rising tide.

BUT REMEMBER that in "he is going up the stairs" we put simply *il monte l'escalier*, because *il monte* means "he goes up", "he does go" or "he is going up". They are all in the Present Tense.

SOMETIMES we can put *en* before a Present Participle. *En* usually means "in" but we can vary the meaning a bit to suit the English.

en arrivant à la gare, on arriving at the station

How to Say "I was giving"

Take the Present Participle *donnant*, drop off the *-ant* and add these endings instead: *-ais, -ais, -ait, -ions, -iez, -aient*. This gives us

THE IMPERFECT TENSE

je donnais, I was giving	*nous donnions*, we were giving
(*tu donnais*, thou wast giving)	*vous donniez*, you were giving
il donnait, he was giving	*ils donnaient*, they were giving

ALL Present Participles end in *-ant*, and the Imperfect Tense of every French verb has these six endings. Of these six, the first three and the last are all pronounced very like the "a" in "day".

"I was giving" is the usual meaning of the Imperfect, but it's not the only one. It also means "I used to give". Thirdly, if we say "I often went to the pictures" we really mean "I often used to go to the pictures". So, whenever, for instance, "went" or "gave" can be turned into "used to go", "used to give" WITHOUT ALTERING THE MEANING, then we use the Imperfect.

COMPARE these two:

(i) I often gave him some money.
(ii) I gave him some money yesterday.

The first refers to a habit, something that "used to happen" often, but the second to something that happened once—yesterday.

So:

(i) *Je lui donnais de l'argent.*
(ii) *Hier je lui ai donné de l'argent.*

In each case the English is "gave", but in the first it can be turned into "used to give"; in the second it cannot. That is the test.

Word List 15

une horloge, clock
voisin(e), neighbour, neighbouring
la mer, the sea
au bord de la mer, at the seaside (*bord*—edge)

bientôt, soon
jusqu'à, until, up to, as far as
ne . . . jamais, never (used like *ne . . . pas*)
gagner, to gain, win, earn
remarquer, to notice

"That" in sentences such as "I was sure *that* he was not here" is *que* (or *qu'*); *que* also means "than" (as well as "whom" or "which").

Exercise 15 (*a*)

Put into English:

1. Allez-vous souvent au bord de la mer? Non, mais quand nous demeurions près de Calais, je passais beaucoup de temps au bord de la mer. 2. En montant dans le train ce matin j'ai vu notre voisin qui parlait au porteur. 3. Nous achetions des légumes au marché, mais maintenant nous les achetons chez Dupont. 4. A qui est cette grande horloge que vous portiez quand je vous ai rencontré hier? 5. Cette vieille femme, qui est assise à une table de ce café-là, me donnait souvent[1] des cadeaux. 6. Si nous marchons jusqu'à l'hôtel, je suis sûr que nous rencontrerons mon voisin: il est toujours là à cette heure. 7. Mon cousin travaillait dans une usine; maintenant il est le propriétaire d'un hôtel au bord de la mer. 8. Avez-vous remarqué l'officier qui traversait la rue pendant que nous allions ce·matin au marché? 9. En arrivant à la gare j'ai acheté deux billets. 10. Si vous marchez avec moi jusqu'au village, je vous montrerai la maison où je demeurais.

---

[1] In French, adverbs such as *souvent*, *hier* are put after the verb; only object pronouns (*le*, *lui*, etc.) and the *ne* (of *ne . . . pas*) can come between the subject of a sentence and the verb.

Exercise 15 (*b*)

Put into French:

1. Where were you going when I met you this morning?
2. I often met the doctor when I was going to school.
3. That little boy has bought three kilogrammes of apples. Did you give him some money yesterday? 4. While I was

going up the stairs I saw someone who was going into your room. 5. My neighbour (*fem.*) is not at home. 6. She was walking towards the station when I looked out of (*par*) my window. 7. Yesterday we made an excursion to the country. 8. During the afternoon we spent two hours in the woods. 9. We used to spend our holidays at the seaside, but now we spend them at my aunt's house. 10. If you do not work while you are at school, you will never earn your living (life). 11. At school that boy never used to work, but now he has more money than his father. 12. We used to meet her often, but when we go to Paris she is never at home.

Have a Try 15

A dix heures quelqu'un a téléphoné au poste de police à Besançon pour annoncer que des voleurs ont pris dans un fourgon (*van*) postal des sacs de lettres et des paquets (*parcels*). La valeur de ces paquets est à présent incertaine, mais elle est probablement grande, parce que Besançon est célèbre pour l'excellence des montres qui sont faites dans cette ville. Beaucoup de montres sont envoyées de Besançon aux magasins d'autres villes en France et il est certain que les voleurs trouveront des montres dans les paquets qu'ils ont pris.

LESSON SIXTEEN

MORE ABOUT "SOME" AND "ANY"

We know already that "some" or "any" is in French *du, de l', de la* or *des*.

du fromage; de l'eau; de l'argent; de la bière; des hommes

But sometimes "some" or "any" is translated in French by *de* whatever the gender of the noun and no matter whether it is singular or plural.

COMPARE these two: "some French wine" and "some good wine". Now *français*, being an adjective of nationality, comes after the noun in French, but *bon*, being a short and common adjective, comes before the noun. This gives us our rule. If the adjective comes AFTER the noun (nationality, colour, long or uncommon adjectives) "some" ("any") is *du, de l', de la* or *des*. If the adjective comes BEFORE the noun then "some" ("any") is *de* (or *d'*).

Examples:

du vin français; but *de bon vin*
des arbres verts, (some) green trees; but *de grands arbres*, (some) tall trees
de l'argent anglais, (some) English money
de belles pommes; but *des pommes rouges*

Provided that one adjective comes before the noun *de* is used, whether another adjective comes after the same noun or not.

de vieux chapeaux—de vieux chapeaux gris; but *des chapeaux gris*

You can have two adjectives both before the noun.

de pauvres petits animaux

If two adjectives both have to come after the noun it is best to put *et* between them.

une foule pittoresque et bruyante, a picturesque and noisy crowd

There is one other instance when this same thing happens.

If the verb is negative (that is used with "not"), then again "some" ("any") is *de* (or *d'*).

We have some money. *Nous avons de l'argent.*
We haven't any (we have no) money. *Nous n'avons pas d'argent.*
Il y a du lait dans la bouteille. There is some milk in the bottle.
Il n'y a pas de lait dans la bouteille. There isn't any milk in the bottle.

How to say "I used to be" and "I used to have".

In the last lesson we saw that the Imperfect Tenses of all verbs have the same endings: *-ais, -ais, -ait, -ions, -iez* and *-aient.*

HERE, then, is the Imperfect of "to have" and also of "to be".

j'avais, I used to have (I had)	*j'étais*, I used to be (I was).
tu avais	*tu étais*
il avait	*il était*
nous avions	*nous étions*
vous aviez	*vous étiez*
ils avaient	*ils étaient*

We saw in Lesson Seven that *j'ai trouvé* can mean either "I have found" or "I found". In Lesson Fifteen we saw that if "I found" really means "I was finding" or "I used to find" we use the Imperfect, *je trouvais.* In the same way, *j'ai été* can mean "I have been" or "I was". But if "I was" really means "I used to be", then we should use *j'étais.*

SIMILARLY "I had" in the sense of "I used to have" or "I was having" is *j'avais*, but "I (have) had" is *j'ai eu* (*eu* is the Past Participle of *avoir*).

J'avais un chien. I had (used to have) a dog.
Hier j'ai eu mal à la tête. Yesterday I had a headache.

Word List 16

monsieur, sir, Mr.
un monsieur, a man, a gentleman
des messieurs, some gentlemen
Madame, madam, Mrs.
mesdames, ladies
mademoiselle, miss, young lady
mesdemoiselles, young ladies
occupé, occupied, taken
payer, to pay, to pay for

M. Blanc, Mr. White
Mme Blanc, Mrs. White
Mlle Blanc, Miss White
une chambre à un (deux) lit(s), a single (double) room
libre, free, vacant
le petit déjeuner, breakfast
aimer, to like, to love

Exercise 16 (*a*)

Put into English:

1. Il y avait de grands arbres et de belles fleurs dans le jardin de la maison où nous demeurions. 2. Si vous n'avez pas d'argent je vous prêterai cinq francs pour acheter du vin rouge. 3. En regardant par ma fenêtre j'ai vu un officier et une douzaine de soldats français qui marchaient vers la gare. 4. Je suis sûr qu'ils allaient monter dans le train qui arrive ici à trois heures. 5. En montant dans l'autobus, j'ai vu notre voisine qui achetait au marché des pommes vertes. 6. Je n'aime pas les pommes vertes. Un jour j'ai mangé un kilogramme de pommes vertes et j'ai passé deux jours au lit. 7. Quand nous étions petits nous allions souvent au bord de la mer. 8. Nous passions nos vacances chez un fermier; il n'avait pas de moutons, mais il avait de très belles vaches. 9. Je suis sûr que cet homme a bu trop de vin: il tombera dans le fleuve. 10. Avez-vous une chambre à un lit qui donne sur la mer? Non, madame, mais nous avons une belle chambre à deux lits qui donne sur le jardin. 11. Cette

place, madame, est occupée, mais il y a ici une chaise qui est libre. 12. Je vous ai dit déjà, M. Dupont, que je n'ai pas d'argent à vous prêter.

Exercise 16 (b)

Put into French:

1. Mr. Green and his wife used to live in our house. Another gentleman, Mr. Black, was their neighbour. 2. We never had any dogs when we were young. 3. We lived in a town and there were many cars in our street. 4. My uncle had some beautiful horses. I used to look at them for (during) hours. 5. The double rooms are occupied, madame, but we have two nice (pretty) single rooms which are free. 6. The two gentlemen who spent the night here have taken the train for Paris this morning. 7. If you do not want to buy these newspapers, miss, I will lend them to Miss Dupont. 8. That good Mr. Dubois has brought you two dozen eggs and some white wine. 9. He told us that he had no money, but this morning he was buying (some) vegetables at the market. 10. If you walk as far as the church, you will meet Mr. and Mrs. Leclerc. 11. There are a crowd of children who are getting into a little boat. 12. Haven't you enough French money (in order) to pay (for) your breakfast?

Have a Try 16

Le directeur de la maison de commerce (*business firm*) où est employé M. Lebrun—le père de Jean—est malade. Pour cette raison M. Lebrun a décidé d'aller à Rouen à (*in*) sa place pour parler d'une affaire importante avec un client qui demeure dans l'ancienne capitale de la Normandie. M. Lebrun a eu la bonne idée d'inviter sa femme et les deux garçons, Jean et Charles, à aller avec lui. Naturellement Charles est très heureux d'accepter cette invitation qui lui donnera l'occasion (*the opportunity*) de visiter Rouen qui est une très belle ville et un centre industriel.

"Il y a un guide parmi les livres qui sont sur la table près de mon lit," dit (*says*) Mme Lebrun. "Je suis sûre que nous trouverons dans ce livre une liste des hôtels à Rouen, et je téléphonerai au bureau d'un des hôtels qui sont recommandés dans mon guide."

LESSON SEVENTEEN

HOW TO SAY "I SHOULD GIVE"

In Lesson Twelve we saw that to get the French for "I shall give" (Future) all we had to do was to add to the Infinitive *donner* the endings *-ai, -as, -a, -ons, -ez, -ont*.

Now in order to be able to say "I should give" all we need to do is to add to the Infinitive *donner* the endings *-ais, -ais, -ait, -ions, -iez, -aient*. Do you recognise these endings? They are exactly the same as those we used in forming the Imperfect. The only difference is that we got the Imperfect by knocking off the *-ant* of the participle *donnant* and adding the endings to the stem *donn-*. BUT to get the Conditional ("I should give") we add them to the Infinitive (just as we added *-ai*, etc., to the Infinitive to form the Future). Here for comparison are all three tenses:

Imperfect	Future	Conditional
je donnais, I was giving.	*je donnerai*, I shall give	*je donnerais* (I should give)
(tu donnais)	*(tu donneras)*	*(tu donnerais)*
il donnait	*il donnera*	*il donnerait*
nous donnions	*noud donnerons*	*nous donnerions*
vous donniez	*vous donnerez*	*vous donneriez*
ils donnaient	*ils donneront*	*ils donneraient*

The Conditional is so called because it is often used to show what would happen or what someone would do under certain conditions.

Si j'avais de l'argent, je vous donnerais un cadeau. If I had some money (but I haven't!) I would give you a present.

We have met the word *si* with the meaning of "so".

si grand, so big

It also means "if".

Meaning "so", *si* is never shortened when followed by a vowel. Meaning "if", it is shortened to *s'* when followed by an "i" but not otherwise.

si énorme, so enormous   *s'il est malade*, if he is ill

67

BUT

si elle est malade, if she is ill

Word List 17

la dame, the lady   *inviter (à)*, to invite (to)
le dîner, dinner   *attraper*, to catch
le poisson, fish   *tirer*, to pull, drag
le fruit, fruit   *penser*, to think
dîner, to dine, have dinner

Exercise 17 (*a*)

Put into English:

1. Si vous êtes si malade, pourquoi avez-vous marché jusqu'au vieux château? 2. Nous allons visiter Mme Dubois. Si elle est chez elle, je l'inviterai à dîner avec nous à l'hôtel. 3. Pour le déjeuner hier nous avons eu du poisson et des fruits. 4. Ce petit garçon a attrapé un poisson si

énorme que j'ai pensé qu'il tomberait dans l'eau pendant qu'il le tirait à la surface. 5. Mme Leroux m'a dit qu'elle me prêterait dix francs pour acheter les billets. 6. Quand le temps était beau nous n'allions jamais au cinéma. 7. S'il ne désirait pas aller au bord de la mer, pourquoi ne l'a-t-il[1]

---

[1] *l'a: l'* = *it*, but in English "so" would be better.

pas dit? 8. Si toutes les places sont occupées, nous monter-
ons dans une autre voiture. 9. Ce monsieur-là est un ami
de mon cousin. Nous l'avons rencontré chez Mme Dupont.
10. Je n'étais pas sûr si vous arriveriez aujourd'hui ou
demain. 11. J'ai dit au fils du médecin qu'il ne gagnerait pas
sa vie, s'il ne travaillait pas à l'école. 12. Il y a une dame à la
porte qui désire parler avec Mme Lepic.

Exercise 17 (b)

Put into French:

1. You will find some fine fish (*plural*) at the market this
morning. 2. The shopkeeper told me that he has no vegetables, but he will bring us some big apples. 3. If I had
enough money, I would invite you to dine at the "White
Horse". 4. That old lady used to be a great actress. 5. No,
madam, there aren't any single rooms which look (give) on
to the sea. 6. I was sure that the policemen would not catch
the men who have stolen your car. 7. If she doesn't want to
go to the cinema, give me her ticket. 8. If she is so rich, why
does she not give fifteen francs to her son? 9. That fish will
pull him into the water if he catches it. 10. This place is
already occupied, sir. If you look (seek), you will find
another chair which is free. 11. How much red wine has he

drunk? Three bottles. 12. We were not sure when we should arrive at the hotel. 13. He would not eat so much, if I was not paying (for) his dinner.

Have a Try 17

En descendant du taxi. M. Lebrun regarde avec anxiété l'horloge de la Gare. "Bon. Nous avons dix minutes avant le départ du train." Il fait (*makes*) un signe à un porteur et les quatre voyageurs lui donnent leurs bagages. Charles remarque avec intérêt que le porteur les attache à une courroie (*strap*) qu'il porte sur les épaules (*shoulders*).

"Nous allons à Rouen," dit (*says*) M. Lebrun, "par le train de onze heures."

"Oui, monsieur. Si vous entrez dans le passage souterrain, je vous chercherai à la barrière."

Au guichet (*booking-office*) M. Lebrun demande quatre billets d'aller et retour de seconde classe. Ils trouvent leur porteur à la barrière.

"A cette heure, monsieur, vous trouverez sans difficulté des places."

En deux minutes ils sont assis dans un compartiment où il n'y a pas d'autres voyageurs. Charles est très content parce qu'il a une place de coin (*corner*). Mme Lebrun n'est pas si contente. Elle regarde son mari d'un air de reproche (*reproach*). "Vous avez donné trop d'argent au porteur. Sommes-nous des touristes américains?"

LESSON EIGHTEEN

ABOUT NUMBERS

We already know (Lesson Eleven) the numbers up to twenty. Here is a further list:

vingt et un, 21	*trente et un*, 31
vingt-deux, 22	*trente-deux*, 32
vingt-trois, 23	*trente-neuf*, 39
vingt-quatre, 24	*quarante*, 40
vingt-cinq, 25	*quarante et un*, 41
vingt-six, 26	*quarante-deux*, 42
vingt-sept, 27	*cinquante*, 50
vingt-huit, 28	*cinquante et un*, 51
vingt-neuf, 29	*soixante*, 60
trente, 30	*soixante et un*, 61

NOTICE that in 21, 31, 41, 51 and 61 we have *et* between the *vingt* (etc.) and the *un*. In all the others there is no *et* but a - linking the two parts together. The *un* in these numbers becomes *une* with a feminine noun, but the other numbers do not alter.

41 bottles, *quarante et une bouteilles*
45 houses, *quarante-cinq maisons*
many houses, *beaucoup de maisons* (*de* after an adverb of quantity)
a dozen men, *une douzaine d'hommes* (*d'* after a noun of quantity)

How to Say "Which house?" or "What book?"

As we know already, "this book" in French is *ce livre* and "that house" is *cette maison*. But how are we to say, for instance, "What book?" or "Which house?" We know that in "the book which I have bought" "which" is *que*: *le livre que j'ai acheté*. But we want to be able to use "which" or "what" before a noun, just as we can translate "this" or "that", "these" and "those" before a noun by using *ce, cet, cette* or *ces*.

HERE are the words we need: "which" or "what" before a masculine noun is *quel* (sing.) or *quels* (plural). "Which" or "what" before a feminine noun is *quelle* (sing.) or *quelles* (plural).

Here are a few examples to show some of the ways in which "what" and "which" can be put into French:

Quel train avez-vous pris? What train did you take (catch)?
Le train qui arrive ici à deux heures. The train which gets here at two o'clock.
A quelle heure allez-vous à l'école? (At) what time do you go to school?
Les fleurs que vous regardez sont des roses. The flowers (which) you are looking at are (some) roses.
De quelles fleurs parlez-vous? Of which flowers are you talking?

Word List 18

le couteau, knife	*couper*, to cut
la salle à manger, dining-room	*la distance*, distance
un auteur, author	*le prix*, price (*also* prize)
préférer, to prefer	*la classe*, class, class-room

Exercise 18 (*a*)

Put into English:

1. Avec quel couteau avez-vous coupé le pain? Avec ce couteau-là. 2. Où est mon journal? Quel journal? Le journal que je vous ai prêté hier. 3. Il y a déjà cinquante voyageurs assis dans la salle à manger de cet hôtel. Allons dîner chez nous. 4. Cet auteur a écrit quarante-sept livres. 5. La maison où nous demeurions était à une distance de vingt-neuf kilomètres de Tours. 6. Si vous allez à Tours vous trouverez douze ou treize grands châteaux à une petite distance de cette ville. 7. J'ai envoyé une carte-postale à mon ami. Il m'a écrit une lettre de trente-deux pages! 8. A quelle heure arriverons-nous à Paris? A trois heures. 9. A quel prix avez-vous acheté ce tableau? Je l'ai payé quarante-deux francs. 10. Quels fruits préférez-vous? J'aime beaucoup les pommes. 11. Combien de garçons y a-t-il dans votre classe? Il y a trente-sept garçons. 12. Avez-vous une bonne place dans votre classe? Oui, très bonne. Je suis assis près de la fenêtre!

Exercise 18 (*b*)

Put into French:

1. In the dining-room of the old castle the table is so big that there are places for forty or fifty men. 2. Which books have you taken? I took the two which were on the table. 3. Let us look for your friend. In which carriage is he? 4. Which books do you prefer? I don't like (the) books which are very long. 5. The farmer told me (said to me) that he has bought fifty-seven cows. 6. At what distance from Paris is your house? At thirty-five kilometres. 7. At which hotel shall we dine? At the "Black Horse". 8. The author of those books which you like used to be one of my friends. 9. I did not see your aunt at the café. At which table was she sitting? 10. At which hotel did you spend the night? At the Grand Hotel, which has a dozen double rooms. 11. At what price did you buy the tickets? At eleven francs. You will find that we have good seats (places). 12. What fish did you eat? I do not like fish; we prefer meat.

Have a Try 18

Pour Charles le voyage de Paris à Rouen n'a pas été long parce qu'il a passé le temps à (*in*) regarder la campagne. Il a remarqué (*noticed*) que les champs en France ne sont pas séparés l'un de l'autre par des haies (*hedges*) et que les femmes et les jeunes filles aident les hommes à cultiver des légumes ou à garder les moutons.

Quand ils arrivent à l'Hôtel Moderne, situé au centre de

la ville, l'employé au bureau (*office*) dit à M. Lebrun qu'il lui
a réservé deux chambres à deux lits et il les invite à entrer
dans l'ascenseur (*lift*). En réponse à une question Mme
Lebrun annonce qu'elle trouve sa chambre très jolie. "Et
vous, Jean ?" "Ah, pour moi, les repas ont plus d'importance
que les chambres !" "Il est une heure," dit M. Lebrun.
"Allons au restaurant."

LESSON NINETEEN

HOW TO SAY "I HAVE SEEN THEM"

In Lesson Eleven we saw that when a past participle is used with any part of the verb "to be" the past participle must agree with the subject of the verb, just as an adjective agrees with its noun.

FOR example:

the door is high, *la porte est haute* (adjective)
the door is shut, *la porte est fermée* (participle)

Fermé is the Past Participle of *fermer* to shut, but here it is feminine (*fermée*) because it is used with *est* and agrees with *la porte*.

In "he has shut the door" we put *il a fermé la porte* because here the participle is used with *a* not *est*.

It is true that a Past Participle when used with any part of *avoir* (to have) does not change to agree with the subject of the sentence, but that is not the whole story. There are times when a Past Participle used with, say, *a* or *avait* does become feminine or plural, and it is very important to know when this happens.

"I saw (have seen) the man" is, of course, *J'ai vu l'homme.* In that sentence "I" is the subject. ("Who saw?" Answer "I") and "the man" is the object ("Saw whom?" Answer "the man").

In the sentence "I saw him" "I" is again the subject, and the object is this time "him" ("Saw whom?" Answer "Him"), and we should put *je l'ai vu*, because the pronoun object "him" must come before the verb.

Now look at these two:

I saw the woman. *J'ai vu la femme.*
I saw her. *Je l'ai vue.*

In each the object is feminine, in the first the noun *la femme*, in the second the pronoun *la* (or *l'*). There doesn't seem much difference, yet in the first sentence we have *vu* and in the second *vue*. WHY? THE REASON is that in the first case the object *la femme* comes AFTER the verb, but in the second the object, being a pronoun, comes BEFORE the verb.

THIS GIVES US OUR RULE: A Past Participle used with any tense of *avoir* (to have) agrees with its DIRECT OBJECT *if* BUT ONLY *if that object is placed* BEFORE *the verb.*

Let's take one or two other sentences:

Where did you buy those shoes? *Où avez-vous acheté ces souliers?* (Object after verb so no agreement.)

I bought them at Dupont's. *Je les ai achetés chez Dupont.* (Object before verb, so Participle agrees.)

I gave her a bicycle. *Je lui ai donné une bicyclette.* (This means "gave a bicycle to her". *Une bicyclette* is the DIRECT OBJECT and *lui*, although coming before the verb, is only the indirect object, and therefore the Participle does not change.)

Have you seen them? *Les avez-vous vus?*

Haven't you seen them? *Ne les avez-vous pas vus?* (In both the direct object is *les* placed before the verb. The fact that there is a *ne . . . pas* in one sentence makes no difference. In each case we must put *vus*.)

Here are further examples:

Leur avez-vous parlé?—Did you speak to them? (No agreement because *leur* is not the direct object.)

Où sont mes livres? Je les ai perdus. Here *les* which refers to *livres* is the direct object, so *perdus* is plural. But in *je ne lui ai pas montré les journaux,* *lui* is the indirect, not the direct object, of *montré.*

Word List 19

le soulier, shoe   *la bicyclette*, bicycle
perdu, lost   *lu*, read

Exercise 19 (*a*)

Put into English:

1. Mme Leroux n'était pas chez elle, mais je l'ai rencontrée devant l'église. 2. Où sont les cartes-postales qui étaient sur cette table? Je les ai données au petit fils du médecin. 3. Je désirais du poisson mais le marchand nous a

envoyé de la viande. 4. Mes journaux ne sont pas ici. Les avez-vous prêtés à quelqu'un? 5. Je cherche ma bicyclette et je ne la trouve pas. Je suis sûr que quelqu'un l'a prise. 6. Les soldats marchaient au château et nous les avons regardés longtemps. 7. Cet auteur a écrit beaucoup de livres, mais je ne les ai pas lus. 8. Ce vieux monsieur et sa femme demeurent près de nous. Je les ai vus mais je ne leur ai jamais parlé. 9. Où sont vos amis? Ne les avez-vous pas vus? 10. Ma tante est très fâchée. Elle a acheté hier des fleurs et mon chien les a mangées. 11. Si vous n'aimez pas cette dame, pourquoi l'avez-vous invitée à dîner? 12. Avez-vous vu mes souliers? Les avez-vous perdus? Les chercherais-je, si je les avais trouvés?

Exercise 19 (*b*)

Put into French:

1. At what time did you meet your aunt? I met her in the street at four o'clock. 2. Those shoes are very big. Where did you buy them? 3. Mme Leroux is very angry because someone has sent her some old fish. 4. I sent it to Mme Leroux because I do not like her. 5. Your uncle and (your) aunt are in Paris. Have you written to them? 6. Where is your bicycle? I have put it behind a tree in the garden.

7. Where are the flowers which were in my room? I have lost them. 8. Why have you not invited your cousins to dinner? I have not invited them because they did not give us any presents. 9. I found some interesting books in that shop near the church. 10. I did not buy them because I hadn't enough money. 11. We used to have a car when we lived in the country, but we have sold it. 12. Are you sure that the door is shut? Yes, I shut it at eight o'clock.

Have a Try 19

A l'école Charles a eu des leçons d'histoire et son professeur lui a parlé de la vie de Jeanne d'Arc. Dans son livre d'histoire aussi Charles a lu avec intérêt de cette jeune fille qui sous l'inspiration des saints qui lui ont parlé a renoncé à (*given up*) la vie tranquille de son village de Domrémy pour aller sauver la France, désolée par l'invasion anglaise. Elle force les Anglais à abandonner le siège d'Orléans, mais bientôt après cette victoire elle tombe entre les mains des Bourguignons (*Burgundians*) qui la livrent (*hand over*) pour une immense somme d'argent à leurs alliés, les Anglais.

Après leur déjeuner à l'Hôtel Moderne Charles et Jean ont visité la tour (*tower*) où Jeanne d'Arc était prisonnière et la Place du Vieux Marché où elle a été brûlée (*burnt*).

LESSON TWENTY

HOW TO SAY "I HAD GIVEN"

We know that *j'avais* (the Imperfect of *avoir*) means "I had", though it can also mean "I was having" or "I used to have". Now, just as we can take the Present *j'ai* and follow it by a Past Participle *j'ai donné* to mean "I have given" (or "I gave"), so we can use *j'avais* (I had) with *donné* (given). Thus *j'avais donné*, I had given. *Nous avions parlé* we had spoken, or *ils avaient vu*, they had seen, and so on.

In the same way, just as we can use the Present of "to be" with a Past Participle *je suis caché*, I am hidden, so we can also use the Imperfect of "to be" with a Past Participle: *l'argent était caché*, the money was hidden.

We must, of course, remember that if it is used with any tense of *être* (to be) the participle agrees with the subject of the verb just as an adjective does.

The door was shut: *La porte était fermée.*
Had you shut the door? *Aviez-vous fermé la porte?*
Yes, I had shut it. *Oui, je l'avais fermée.* (Participle is feminine because it is used with a part of *avoir* and must agree with the object pronoun which comes in front of it.)

How to Say "This one" or "That one"

We know already how to put "this", "that", "these" or "those" into French when each of these words is followed by a noun.

ce chapeau, this hat; *cet homme,* this man; *cette vache,* this cow; *ces soldats (maisons),* these soldiers (houses)

We know, too, that if we want to distinguish between "this" and "that" we can do so by putting *-ci* (short for *ici*—here) or *-là* (there) after the noun.

This book belongs to me, but that book belongs to him. *Ce livre-ci est à moi, mais ce livre-là est à lui.*

BUT SURELY, in English, we should be much more likely to say "This book belongs to me, but that one belongs to him"? In other words, we want to know the French for "this" (one) without having to repeat the noun "book". We can do it like this:

"This (that) one" standing for a masculine noun is *celui*.
"This (that) one" standing for a feminine noun is *celle*.
"These (those) ones" standing for a masculine noun is *ceux*.
"These (those) ones" standing for a feminine noun is *celles*.

Examples:

This book belongs to me, that one belongs to him. *Ce livre-ci est à moi, celui-là est à lui.*
My house is the one which has a green door. *Ma maison est celle qui a une porte verte.*
Those men are soldiers, these are policemen. *Ces hommes-là sont des soldats: ceux-ci sont des agents de police.*

Word List 20

une personne, a person	*jeter*, to throw
des personnes, some people	*reçu*, received
une brique, a brick	*que*, than

Exercise 20 (*a*)

Put into English:

1. Mon cousin désirait acheter ma vieille bicyclette, mais je l'avais vendue déjà. 2. J'étais sûr que quelqu'un avait pris mes souliers, parce que je les ai cherchés dans toutes les chambres. 3. Le marchand était très fâché parce que de méchants garçons avaient jeté des briques dans la rue. 4. Ils avaient cassé douze bouteilles de bière qu'il allait envoyer à l'hôtel. 5. Je vous ai dit que ces souliers-ci sont à moi: ceux-là sont au monsieur qui est assis à la table près de la fenêtre. 6. J'ai acheté ce livre-ci parce qu'il est plus intéressant que celui-là. 7. Il y a dix personnes dans cette voiture: montons dans celle-ci, où nous trouverons des places libres. 8. Nous avons visité beaucoup de châteaux, mais nous préférons celui-ci parce qu'il est plus beau que

tous les autres. 9. Quel tableau préférez-vous? Celui-ci ou celui que je vous ai apporté? 10. Nous n'étions pas sûrs dans quel train vous arriveriez—le train de deux heures ou celui que vous avez pris hier. 11. La bicyclette verte n'est pas à moi, mais je vous prêterai celle-ci. 12. Où sont vos souliers? Je les ai perdus: mon cousin m'a donné ceux-ci.

Exercise 20 (b)

Put into French:

1. Who was that lady? Which lady? That one who was looking at the flowers. 2. In which house used you to live? In that one. It has a nice garden, but the rooms were very small. 3. Of these two books, we prefer this one, because I have read the other. 4. Let us get into (*monter*) this carriage: there are two dogs and five children in that one. 5. I was sure that I had never seen that old lady. But this one, who is crossing the road, is a friend of my aunt. 6. This is the window which is broken. Look at it! 7. Had you not read in the newspaper that the queen was going to spend a week at the castle? 8. Which castle? The (that) one, which I showed you when we made an excursion. 9. There are fifty people in this hotel and all the tables are occupied. No, this

one is free. 10. I told (said to) my sister that I had written
her a long letter, but she has not received it. 11. These cows
and those belong to my uncle. We used to have some cows
but we have sold them. 12. Are you the naughty little boy
who threw this brick? No, madam. I threw that one.

Have a Try 20

Charles, qui était fatigué, a passé une bonne nuit. Jean et
sa mère sont déjà dans la salle à manger de l'hôtel et
Charles arrive au moment où le garçon apporte le petit
déjeuner qui consiste en (*of*) une bonne tasse de café ou de
chocolat avec du pain et du beurre normand. C'est un repas
moins substantiel que le petit déjeuner anglais, mais en
France on (*one*) a le déjeuner une heure plus tôt qu' (*earlier
than*) en Angleterre.

LESSON TWENTY-ONE

THE USE OF C'EST

We know that *il est* means "he is" and sometimes "it is". For instance, "it is certain that he is not here", *il est certain qu'il n'est pas ici.* But in French "it is" is frequently translated as *c'est.* This happens, for instance, when "it is" is followed by a personal pronoun.

It is you whom I saw. *C'est vous que j'ai vu.*

REMEMBER that *je* can be used only as the subject of a verb. If there is no verb we must use *moi*: just as we do after a preposition—*avec moi*, with me (see Lesson Twelve) so:

   it is I, *c'est moi*   it is he, *c'est lui*

BUT *c'est* can also be used followed by a noun, and in this case it can mean, if necessary, "he (she) is".

Who is at the door? It is a man whom I have never seen. *Qui est à la porte? C'est un homme que je n'ai jamais vu.*

He is an extraordinary man! *C'est un homme extraordinaire!* (*C'est* is turned into *est-ce* in questions.)

Who is there? Is it you, Charles? Yes, it is I. *Qui est là? Est-ce vous, Charles? Oui, c'est moi.* (*C'est* can be used followed by an adjective, but the "it" usually refers to something already mentioned.)

Have you done your work? Yes, it isn't difficult. *Avez-vous fait votre travail? Oui, ce n'est pas difficile.*

How to Say "I shall have" and "I should have"

We know already (Lesson Twelve) that the Future Tenses of all verbs have the same ending: *-ai, -as, -a, -ons, -ez* and *-ont.* Usually we can get the Future by adding these endings to the Infinitive of the verb: *je donnerai, je trouverai* and so on. BUT there are a few verbs which don't follow this rule. Among these is *avoir.* Here is its Future:

j'aurai, I shall have	*nous aurons*, we shall have
(*tu auras*)	*vous aurez*, you will have
il aura, he will have	*ils auront*, they will have

In the same way, we know that the Conditional (I should) of every verb ends in: *-ais, -ais, -ait, -ions, -iez, -aient.* Usually we form the Conditional by adding these endings to the Infinitive: *je donnerais, je trouverais.*

AGAIN, there are exceptions. One of them is *avoir* and to get the Conditional we alter it in exactly the same way as we did when forming the Future.

j'aurais, I should have	*nous aurions*, we should have
(*tu aurais*)	*vous auriez*, you would have
il aurait, he would have	*ils auraient*, they would have

Word List 21

su, known	*le moment*, the moment	*vite*, quickly

Exercise 21 (*a*)

Put into English:

1. Je n'ai pas pris vos dix francs: c'est cet enfant-là qui les a trouvés. 2. Si j'avais su que vos amis allaient arriver par le train de dix heures je les aurais rencontrés à la gare. 3. Si vous me prêtez deux francs j'aurai assez d'argent pour acheter du poisson et des fruits pour le déjeuner. 4. Qui est ce monsieur? C'est l'oncle de Jean. C'est lui qui a acheté notre vieille voiture. 5. Qui est ce jeune homme-là? Celui-là? C'est un touriste américain. 6. Quel livre achetez-vous? C'est un livre de l'auteur que nous avons rencontré chez M. Leriche. C'est très intéressant. 7. Regardez ces arbres-là. Nous aurons de belles pommes. 8. J'aurais eu de beaux fruits dans mon jardin, si votre petit neveu ne les avait pas volés. 9. Je n'aime pas ce monsieur. C'est lui qui a fermé la porte du compartiment au moment où (*when*) je désirais monter dans le train. 10. Est-ce derrière cet arbre-ci que vous avez mis votre bicyclette? 11. Je vous aurais écrit si j'avais su dans quel hôtel vous passiez vos vacances. 12. Ma tante ne voyage jamais en avion: elle pense que c'est dangereux.

Exercise 21 (*b*)

Put into French:

1. Of these two pictures it is this one that we prefer.
2. Have you enough money (in order) to buy some vegetables? 3. Did you see that young lady? She is the daughter
of our neighbour. 4. If I had known at what time (*heure*)
your train would arrive I would not have walked so quickly
to the station. 5. It is not at this hotel, but at that one, that
we shall meet you tomorrow. 6. Is it he, or his sister, who
(has) won all the prizes? 7. He is an extraordinary man. He
has an aeroplane and two big cars, but he travels always by
(*à*) bicycle. 8. Tomorrow for our breakfast we shall have
cups of coffee with some bread and (some) butter. 9. Do not
let us get into that compartment. In this one there are four
places which are vacant. 10. Do not walk so near the water.
It's dangerous. 11. He is an excellent doctor, but we don't
like him much. 12. I shall not work in this factory. I should
have too much work.

Have a Try 21

Pendant que M. Lebrun visite un client, Jean et Charles
sont en promenade (*on a walk*) dans la ville. Mme Lebrun a
prêté son guide à son fils et Charles a acheté un plan de
Rouen. Ils arrivent sans difficulté à la Place Notre Dame,
où est située la cathédrale. "Regardez ces deux grandes
tours," dit Jean. "Celle-ci est La Tour St. Romain, celle-là
est la Tour de Beurre." "De Beurre! Pourquoi? C'est
extraordinaire." Jean consulte son guide. "Ah, oui. Le
monsieur qui a écrit ce livre nous donne l'explication. Dans
le bon vieux temps (*plural in English*) il (*it*) était défendu
(*forbidden*) aux Catholiques de manger du beurre en Carême
(*Lent*), mais l'évêque (*bishop*) a déclaré que les personnes
qui lui donneraient de l'argent pour la construction de cette
Tour auraient sa permission de (*to*) manger du beurre en

Carême." "C'est très intéressant," dit Charles, "mais si je donnais mon argent cette tour aurait reçu le nom (*name*) de la Tour de Chocolat!"

LESSON TWENTY-TWO

HOW TO TELL THE TIME IN FRENCH

There are three words which mean "time" in French, and we must distinguish between them.

Fois (fem.) means "time" in the sense of "once", "twice", "three times".

une fois, deux fois, trois fois and so on.

Temps (masc.) means "time" in a general sense.

longtemps, (for) a long time
Le temps passait vite. The time was quickly passing. (It also means "weather".)
Le temps était beau. The weather was fine.

Heure (fem.) means the "time of day", "o'clock" or "hour".

Il est trois heures. It is three o'clock.
Quelle heure est-il? What time is it?
Je l'ai cherché pendant trois heures. I looked for him for three hours.

The French for "minute" is *minute* (fem.), but the simplest method is to leave it out.

From the hour up to half-past the hour we have only to give the hour, and follow this with the number of minutes so:

ten minutes past three, *trois heures dix*
twenty-five minutes past ten, *dix heures vingt-cinq*

For "a quarter-past one" we could in the same way put *une heure quinze*, but we could put instead *une heure et quart*, one o'clock and quarter.

For "half-past two" we could put *deux heures trente* (2.30), but there is also *deux heures et demie*. *Demi(e)* means "half" and is made feminine because "half" here means "half (an hour)" and *heure* is a feminine noun.

From the half hour until the next hour, we use *moins*, less. When in English we say "twenty minutes to two" the French method is to turn this into "two hours less (or 'minus') twenty": *deux heures moins vingt*. SIMILARLY "five minutes to three" becomes "three hours less five"—*trois heures moins cinq*.

For "twelve o'clock" it is usual to use *midi* (midday) and *minuit* (midnight).

Il est midi dix. It is ten minutes past twelve.
Il est minuit moins dix. It is ten minutes to twelve (at night).

IN ENGLISH we say "three o'clock IN the afternoon" or "eleven AT night". The French use *de* NOT *dans*.

trois heures de l'après-midi; onze heures de la nuit

How to Say "I shall be" and "I should be"

Just as "I shall have" is *j'aurai* and "I should have" is *j'aurais*, the verb *être* (to be) is exceptional in the Future and Conditional. Instead of adding the vowel endings to the Infinitive we put *ser* instead of *être* and then add the endings.

je serai, I shall be	*je serais*, I should be
(tu seras)	*(tu serais)*
il sera	*il serait*
nous serons	*nous serions*
vous serez	*vous seriez*
ils seront	*ils seraient*

Word List 22

la représentation, the performance	*pardon*, excuse me
le théâtre, theatre	*s'il vous plaît*, please
aimable, kind, amiable	*merci*, thank you
le soir, the evening	*le chocolat*, chocolate
commencer, to begin	*Angleterre* (fem.), England

Exercise 22 (a)

Put into English:

1. Je vous ai dit deux fois que je serai au marché à deux heures et demie si le temps est beau. 2. Marchons vite, nous n'avons pas beaucoup de temps. Il est déjà trois

heures moins vingt (*minutes*). 3. La représentation commencera à huit heures du soir, mais je vous rencontrerai devant le théâtre à sept heures et quart. 4. Pardon, monsieur, quelle heure est-il, s'il vous plaît? 5. Il est neuf heures moins quinze, madame. Merci, monsieur. 6. Cette jeune fille est très aimable. J'allais monter dans ce train-là, mais elle m'a dit que notre train ne sera pas ici avant onze heures vingt-cinq. 7. Il est deux heures moins cinq à (*by*) ma montre. Nous aurons le temps d' (*to*) acheter des journaux et des cartes postales. 8. Marchez plus vite, s'il vous plaît. Il sera déjà minuit quand nous arriverons[1] chez nous. 9. En Angleterre nous avons le déjeuner à une heure, mais si vous passez vos vacances en France vous aurez le déjeuner à midi. 10. Si vous montez dans ce train vous serez à Paris à six heures et quart. 11. Je les aurais rencontrés si j'avais su à quelle heure ils seraient à la gare. 12. Est-il déjà midi? Non, il est onze heures et demie.

Exercise 22 (*b*)

Put into French:

1. It is half-past three. I thought (that) she would be here before two o'clock. 2. I have seen her twice, but I have never spoken to her. 3. At what time will you be at the station? At a quarter to four. 4. The performance will not begin before half-past eight in (of) the evening. 5. If we arrive at the theatre at twenty minutes to eight we shall have the time to (*d'*) buy some fruit and some chocolate. 6. Excuse me, sir, what time is it, please? It is twenty-past ten, madam. 7. We shall not have enough time (in order) to visit the castle. It is already ten minutes to twelve (midday). 8. We shall not be home before midnight if we do not walk more quickly. 9. What time was it when you saw her yesterday? It was ten minutes to six. 10. I thought that the shops would

---

[1] In English "we arrive", but the sense is really "will arrive", and with *quand* in such cases the French use the Future not the Present.

be shut, because it was already half-past five. 11. How many
times have you been to Paris? Three or four times. It's a
lovely city (town). 12. How much time did you spend at the
doctor's (house)? We were at his house from three o'clock
until a quarter to four.

Have a Try 22

A onze heures et quart, Mme Lebrun et les deux garçons
sont au bord de la mer. Après le petit déjeuner ils ont
marché à la gare où ils ont pris le rapide (*express*) qui les a
amenés (*brought*) en très peu de temps à Dieppe. Là ils
montent dans un des autobus qui assurent le service entre
Dieppe et le Tréport et ils descendent de l'autobus à une
jolie petite plage (*beach*).

Jean et Charles regardent avec satisfaction l'eau claire et
calme. En cinq minutes ils sont en maillot (*bathing-dress*).

Jean indique un rocher (*rock*) qui perce (*pierces*) la surface
de l'eau à une distance de trente mètres (*yards, metres*).

"Je gage (*bet*) que j'arriverai à ce rocher avant vous," dit-il.

Les deux garçons commencent à nager (*swim*) de toutes leurs forces. La tête plongée dans l'eau, Charles ne remarque pas un vieux monsieur devant lui et entre en collision violente avec lui. Quand il lui a fait ses excuses Jean est assis déjà sur le rocher.

LESSON TWENTY-THREE

HOW TO SAY "I HAVE COME"

Now and then, in the Bible or even in modern books, we may come across phrases such as "he is gone" or "the time is come", instead of the usual "has gone" or "has come".

Anyway, the point is that there are certain verbs in French where we have to use, say, *est* not *a* before the Past Participle. Most of these, though not all, are verbs of motion, that is to do with coming, going, falling and so on.

HERE are the Past Participles of some of these verbs with which we must remember to use, for instance, *je suis*, and not *j'ai*, even though the English is "I have" not "I am".

Some of them we know already.

allé, gone	*tombé*, fallen
parti, departed, set out (for)	*venu*, come
monté, gone up, got into	*revenu*, come back
descendu, gone down, descended	*entré*, entered, went into
devenu, become	*resté*, remained
arrivé, arrived	

We must remember, too, that if we use *est* not *a* before a Past Participle the participle must agree, like an adjective, with the subject of the verb. The following examples will show what we have to do:

He has shut the door. *Il a fermé la porte.*
The door is shut. *La porte est fermée.*

In the first we use *a* because the verb is not one of the ones in the list above. In the second we naturally use *est* because the English is "is".

BUT:

He has gone (*or* he went) to the pictures. *Il est allé au cinéma.*
They arrived at the station. *Ils sont arrivés à la gare.*

In the same way, of course, we must use *était* not *avait* for "had" before these same participles.

I had not seen her. *Je ne l'avais pas vue.*
She had fallen into the water. *Elle était tombée dans l'eau.*
She would have fallen. *Elle serait tombée.*

How to Say "First", "Second" and so on

We know already the French numbers, one, two, three up to sixty or so. We need also to be able to say "the first" "the second" and so on.

The French for "first" is *premier*. This is an adjective and its feminine, like those of other words ending in *-er*, is formed by changing this into *-ère*: *cher* (dear)—*chère*; *le premier—la première*.

IN ENGLISH we usually add "th" to the number—"seventh", "nine"—"ninth", dropping the final "e" (if there is one) before adding the "th".

IN FRENCH, in the same way, we add *-ième*: *trois—le (la) troisième*, third; *quatre—le (la) quatrième*, fourth.

In numbers from 17 upwards, when the number is made up of two words, we add *-ième* to the second only: 20th, *le vingtième*; 21st, *le vingt et unième*; 22nd, *le vingt-deuxième*.

There is no need to give a list of all the numbers. But here are a few, including those in which a slight alteration in spelling is made in changing the (cardinal) number into the ordinal (that is one which indicates the order, 3rd, 4th, 5th).

first, *le premier (la première)*   eleventh, *le (la) onzième*[3]
second, *le (la) deuxième*   seventeenth, *le (la) dix-septième*
fifth, *le (la) cinquième*   fifty-fifth, *le cinquante-cinquième*
ninth, *le (la) neuvième*[1]

Word List 23

un étage, a floor   *la cave*, cellar   *la clef*,[2] key

---

[1] NOTE that the "f" of *neuf* is softened into a "v" (*neuvième*), as with "hoof", "hooves" in English.
[2] By exception le (la) is NOT shortened into *l'* before *onze* or *onzième*.
[3] Pronounced rather like "clay" in English.

Exercise 23 (*a*)

Put into English:

1. Non, monsieur, Mme Dupont n'est pas chez elle. Elle est partie ce matin pour la campagne. 2. Si ces petits garçons n'étaient pas montés dans ce mauvais petit bateau ils ne seraient pas tombés dans l'eau. 3. Hier nous sommes allés à Paris pour la première fois. 4. Notre hôtel est très grand. Nous avons une belle chambre au quatrième étage. 5. Elle allait passer ses vacances au bord de la mer, mais elle est revenue à Paris après cinq jours. 6. A l'école elle était toujours la première de sa classe, mais elle est devenue très paresseuse. 7. Nous avons fait une belle excursion, mais ma tante, qui était malade, est restée à l'hôtel. 8. Le propriétaire est descendu à la cave pour chercher une bouteille de vin blanc. 9. Si vous aviez marché plus vite, nous serions arrivés chez nous à l'heure du déjeuner. 10. Quand je suis arrivé chez M. Dubois, sa sœur m'a dit qu'il était parti déjà pour Bordeaux. 11. C'est le dixième jour de nos vacances. C'est aussi le neuvième jour de mauvais temps! 12. Elle ne nous a pas dit qu'elle était revenue par avion.

Exercise 23 (*b*)

Put into French:

1. At what time did she arrive at your house? At midnight. 2. I had gone up to my room on the seventh floor. 3. He has gone to Paris, but his sister has remained at home. 4. We went into the hotel, but our friends had departed already for the seaside. 5. We live in the first house in (of) the street. It has a green door. 6. I have bought three tickets for the second performance of this evening. It begins at half-past eight. 7. We would not have come back if we had known that you were not at home (use *chez*). 8. When we arrived at the station, the train had already left (departed). 9. The police went down to the cellar, where they

found two young thieves who were hidden behind the
bottles. 10. Mme Dupont is very angry. She went up as far
as the ninth floor and on (*en*) arriving at her door she found
that she had lost her key. 11. When I saw her for the first
time she was young. Now she has become very old.
12. When did they return (have they returned) from the
seaside? They arrived home (use *chez*) yesterday at half-
past seven.

Have a Try 23

A Paris il y a beaucoup de maisons qui n'ont pas d'ascenseur. Pour cette raison une personne qui occupe un appartement (*flat*) au premier étage est en général dans la nécessité
de payer un loyer (*rent*) plus considérable que le locataire
(*tenant, occupant*) d'un appartement au sixième.

M. Billot n'était pas riche et c'est pourquoi l'appartement
où il passait sa vieillesse était au septième étage. Le vieux
monsieur avait dans sa chambre une horloge de parquet
(*grandfather clock*). Un jour il a remarqué avec regret que
cette horloge qu'il aimait beaucoup ne marchait pas bien.
Un horloger est venu emporter (*take away, carry off*)
l'horloge pour la réparer.

Cinq jours après un homme est descendu d'une voiture
de livraison (*delivery*) devant la maison et a commencé à

monter l'escalier, en portant l'horloge qui était maintenant
en bon état (*state, condition*). A ce moment un jeune homme,
qui demeurait aussi dans la maison, a vu le porteur qui
montait avec difficulté parce que la grande horloge était
très lourde (*heavy*). "Mon ami," lui dit-il d'un air innocent.
"Si vous désirez savoir (*know*) l'heure, pourquoi ne portez-
vous pas une montre? Ce serait beaucoup plus simple!"

LESSON TWENTY-FOUR

HOW TO SAY "WHICH ONE?" OR "WHICH OF?"

We know that "this" before a noun is *ce, cet* or *cette* and that "this one" (Lesson Twenty) is *celui* or *celle*.

cette maison; ma maison est celle-ci

We also know that "which (what)" followed by a noun is *quel(s)* (masc.) or *quelle(s)* (fem.).

Quelle heure est-il? What time is it?

BUT how are we to say "which one, etc."?
For this we use *lequel*, and as it is made up of the article *le* and *quel*, it can, although written in one word, have the following forms: *lequel, laquelle, lesquels* and *lesquelles*.

We can even have *duquel, de laquelle, desquel(le)s* or *auquel, à laquelle* and *auxquel(le)s*, but we need not bother about most of these here.

REMEMBER that *quel* is used with a noun, while *lequel* stands instead of one (just as with *ce* and *celui*).

Quels livres avez-vous pris? Which books have you taken?
Lequel de ces deux livres avez-vous acheté? Which of these two books have you bought?
Dans quelle maison est-il entré? Into which house did he go?
Dans laquelle de ces maisons est-il entré? Into which of these houses did he go?
Auquel de ces deux garçons avez-vous prêté ma bicyclette? To which of these two boys did you lend my bicycle?

How to Say "Bigger" and "Biggest"

When we use words such as "bigger" we are using what is called the "comparative", because something is bigger (or smaller) than or in comparison with something else. We can say "larger" or "thinner", but not, for instance, "interestinger" or "intelligenter". Instead we say, of course, "more interesting", "more intelligent". In French we use *plus* (more) not only with longer words such as *intéressant* but with short ones such as *grand* or *vieux*.

My car is bigger than that one. *Ma voiture est plus grande que celle-là.*

SOMETIMES the French will use *moins* (less) in the same way.

He is less intelligent (more stupid) than his brother. *Il est moins intelligent (plus bête) que son frère.*

BUT there are a few adjectives which have a special comparative form in French. Just as we say "better" NOT "more good", so the French say *meilleur* NOT *plus bon*.

Ces livres sont meilleurs que ceux-là. These books are better than those.

If we want to say "biggest" in French, all we have to do is to put *le (la, les)* before the French for "bigger".

plus grand becomes *le plus grand*
la plus grande maison, the biggest house

It follows that as *meilleur* is "better", "best" is *le meilleur* (WITHOUT *plus*).

les meilleurs hôtels, the best hotels

Exercise 24 (a)

Put into English:

1. Laquelle de ces deux bicyclettes est à vous? Celle-ci est à moi. 2. Le monsieur à qui j'ai vendu ma voiture est parti pour la campagne. 3. Auquel de ces messieurs avez-vous prêté mon journal? A celui-là. 4. Le couteau avec lequel vous avez coupé le pain est meilleur que celui-ci. 5. Les chambres au cinquième étage sont plus petites que celles du premier, mais elles sont moins chères. 6. De tous les hôtels de cette ville l'Hôtel de la Gare est le plus grand, mais au Cheval Blanc les repas sont meilleurs. 7. Mme Chose est plus jeune que ma tante, mais elle est beaucoup moins aimable. 8. Il y a cinquante-cinq chambres dans cet

hôtel. Laquelle est celle de vos amis? 9. Cet auteur a écrit beaucoup de livres. Lequel préférez-vous? 10. Le propriétaire m'a donné deux clefs. Laquelle est celle de votre chambre? 11. J'ai vu un voleur qui entrait par une fenêtre dans une de ces maisons: mais laquelle? 12. Notre voisin est plus riche que nous: il voyage en première classe et dans les hôtels il a toujours la meilleure chambre.

Exercise 24 (b)

Put into French:

1. We have two rooms which are free. Which do you prefer? 2. Into which of these two rooms have you put my suitcase? Into that one, madam. 3. To which of these girls did you give my key? 4. To which of these two boys did you lend my knife? 5. The castle which we visited yesterday is bigger than this one. 6. If you go to the Station Hotel you will have a nice room, but the meals here are much better. 7. We have sold the house in which we used to live. 8. There are many cafés in this town. Into which did he go? 9. The horse is cleverer than the sheep, but the elephant is the most intelligent of all the animals. 10. Of which man were you speaking? Of the doctor. 11. Of which of these two gentlemen were you speaking? Of that one. 12. The town to which he has gone is near the sea.

Have a Try 24

"Où allez-vous passer vos vacances, mon ami?" "A Paris. Ce sera ma première visite." "En ce cas (*case*) je vous conseille (*advise*) de loger dans un hôtel près de la Place St. Michel." "Pourquoi?" "Parce que dans cette partie de la ville il y a des hôtels où vous trouverez tout le confort que vous désirez à un prix raisonnable." "Oui, mais je serais à une distance considérable du centre de Paris et si je suis forcé de monter dans un taxi pour aller à la Cathédrale, au Louvre ou aux grands magasins, je n'aurai pas assez

d'argent pour payer ma chambre à l'hôtel ou mes repas dans
un restaurant." "Mais non, il y a un excellent service
d'autobus et vous avez aussi le Métropolitain" (*Underground*).

LESSON TWENTY-FIVE

ABOUT "MYSELF"

We know that when a pronoun is the object of a verb it must come before that verb.

Thus "the thief hides his money", *le voleur cache son argent*, but "he hides it" is *il le cache*. Now *il le cache* might also mean "he hides him", as for instance, when someone helps an escaping prisoner by concealing him from his pursuers. The *il* refers to one person, the *le* to another. But the escaping prisoner might, for instance, seek to throw his pursuers off the scent by his own efforts. He might think, "I will hide myself behind that tree" (while they go by). In "I hide him" the subject "I" represents one person and "him" another: *je le cache*. But in "I hide myself" the subject "I" and the object "myself" are both the same person, namely, "me". We therefore put *je me cache*. "We hide ourselves" would be *nous nous cachons*. But how are we to say "he hides himself"? We can't put *il le cache*, because that means that "he (one person) hides him (somebody else)". So in the third person we have to use a new object pronoun *se*. This can mean either "himself", "herself", "themselves" or, with the Infinitive, "oneself". Thus *se cacher* is "to hide oneself", and its Present Tense, in full, would be:

Je me cache, I hide myself   *nous nous cachons*, we hide ourselves.
(tu te caches)   *vous vous cachez*
il (elle) se cache   *ils se cachent*

We can use *se* also as the indirect object of a verb. For instance, "I will give him a present". This really means "I will give a present (direct object) to him (indirect object)" *Je lui donnerai un cadeau*. But you can buy presents for yourself as well as other people. So we can put:

I will give myself a present. *Je me donnerai un cadeau.*

and

She will give herself a present. *Elle se donnera un cadeau.*

SOMETIMES a French verb must be used with an object when we can leave it out in English. For instance "That small boy never washes (himself)". In French the *se* must be put in: *Ce petit garçon ne se lave jamais.* Again, *arrêter* means "to arrest", but *s'arrêter* means "to stop".

The policeman arrests the thief. *L'agent de police arrête le voleur.*
The train does not stop here. *Le train ne s'arrête pas ici.*

Days and Months

HERE are the days of the week:

(*le*) *dimanche*, Sunday	(*le*) *jeudi*, Thursday
(*le*) *lundi*, Monday	(*le*) *vendredi*, Friday
(*le*) *mardi*, Tuesday	(*le*) *samedi*, Saturday
(*le*) *mercredi*, Wednesday	

HERE are the months of the year:

(*le*) *janvier*, January	(*l'*) *août*, August
(*le*) *février*, February	(*le*) *septembre*, September
(*le*) *mars*, March	(*l'*) *octobre*, October
(*l'*) *avril*, April	(*le*) *novembre*, November
(*le*) *mai*, May	(*le*) *décembre*, December
(*le*) *juin*, June	*le mois*, month
(*le*)*juillet*, July	

Here, just as a matter of interest, is the French for certain special days:

Le jour de l'an, New Year's Day
(*Le*) *mardi gras*, Shrove Tuesday
(*Le*) *mercredi des Cendres*, Ash Wednesday
(*Le*) *dimanche de Pâques*, Easter Sunday
(*Le*) *Noël*, Christmas
La veille de Noël, Christmas Eve

NOTE

(1) Days and months are written in French with a small NOT a capital letter.

(2) In dates use *premier* for the 1st of the month, but *deux*, *trois* and so on for all the others.

(3) Do not translate "on" before days of the week or "of" in dates of the months.

on Monday, the first of July, *lundi le premier juillet*
on Wednesday, the ninth of April, *mercredi le neuf avril*

THERE is no need to learn all these days and months at once: turn to the list and after a while you will find that you know them.

Word List 25

(se) blesser, to wound (oneself)
s'habiller, to dress, get dressed
s'approcher(de), to approach, draw near (to)

la voie, (railway) track, line
prudent, prudent, careful
l'herbe (fem.), grass
jeter, to throw

Exercise 25 (*a*)

Put into English:

1. Le train s'arrête parce qu'une vieille vache est assise sur

la voie: il y a des voyageurs qui sont très fâchés 2. Lundi, le premier janvier nous sommes allés au théâtre. 3. Jeudi le vingt-huit juillet nous sommes partis par avion pour la France. 4. Ne traversez pas la voie au moment où un train s'approche. 5. Le chasseur n'a pas tué le tigre. Il l'a blessé et le pauvre animal se cache dans l'herbe. 6. Le cinq novembre les agents de police ont arrêté beacoup de personnes qui jetaient des pétards (*squibs*) dans la rue. 7. Si vous tombez dans cette eau profonde, vous vous tuerez. 8. Du vingt août jusqu'au six septembre je serai au bord de la mer avec mon père. 9. Quand êtes-vous revenus de Paris? Nous sommes arrivés chez nous samedi le trente juillet. 10. Si vous ne vous habillez pas vite, vous n'aurez pas de petit déjeuner. 11. Si nous nous cachons dans la cave ils ne nous trouveront pas. 12. Si vous n'êtes pas prudent vous vous blesserez. Ces grands couteaux-là sont dangereux.

Exercise 25 (b)

Put into French:

1. If the train does not stop at this little station we will walk as far as the town. 2. (On) Thursday we do not go to (the) school and our holidays will begin (on) the fifteenth of December. 3. If you throw those squibs (*pétards*) you will wound someone. 4. You will kill yourself if you are not careful. 5. A sheep has been killed, because it was crossing the line while the train was approaching. 6. I am sure that those boys have not gone to school. Where are they hiding? 7. The dog has hidden the fish in my aunt's bed. She will be very angry! 8. (On) Friday, the 13th (of) June we shall be in Paris. 9. We dress very quickly when we are at the seaside. 10. My sister departed for London on the first of April and she came back here on the second of May. 11. Excuse me, madame, the trains do not stop here. This station is shut. 12. She will wound herself if she is not careful.

Have a Try 25

"Vous m'avez dit qu'à Paris il est possible d'aller sans difficulté par autobus de la Place St. Michel, par exemple, jusqu'à la Place de l'Opéra!"

"Oui. C'est très simple et, si vous achetez un carnet (*booklet*) de billets, vous trouverez que ce sera moins cher que (*than*) d'acheter un billet chaque (*each*) fois que vous montez dans un autobus. Si vous allez par le Métropolitain, il est possible de changer de train une ou deux fois et votre billet reste valable (*valid, usable*) jusqu'au moment où vous montez à la surface.

"A l'entrée d'une station du Métro il y a toujours un plan qui marque toutes les lignes et je suis certain que vous n'aurez pas de difficulté à trouver s'il est nécessaire ou non de changer de train pour arriver à votre destination."

LESSON TWENTY-SIX

HOW TO SAY "I SELL"

Most verbs in French have the ending *-er* in the Infinitive. But there are some which end in *-re: vend-re*, to sell; *descendre*, to go down.

HERE is the Present Tense of *vendre*:

je vends, I sell	*nous vendons*, we sell
(tu vends)	*vous vendez*
il vend	*ils vendent*

You will see that the three plural endings are exactly the same as in the same tense of *donner*.

All Present Participles end in *-ant: vendant*, selling.

To form the Imperfect we have, as with other verbs, only to drop off the *-ant* and replace it with *-ais, -ais, -ait, -ions, -iez* and *-aient*.

je vendais, I was selling, I used to sell, I sold	*nous vendions*, we were selling, we used to sell, we sold
(tu vendais)	*vous vendiez*
il vendait	*ils vendaient*

The Past Participle is *vendu*. So:

j'ai vendu, I (have) sold

More about Object Pronouns

We know that object pronouns must come before the verb (Lesson Twelve). The pronoun may be the direct object or the indirect object.

Je l'ai vu. I saw him (direct object).
Je lui ai donné de l'argent. I gave him some money. I gave some money (direct object) to him (indirect object).

Now if we say instead "I gave it to him" we get both the direct object "it" and the indirect object "to him" in the same sentence. In "He gave it (direct object) to us" (indirect object) the same applies. Both object pronouns must come in front of the verb, but in what order? Which do we put first? Fortunately, it's quite simple. This is the rule. With two object pronouns, put the indirect before the direct *except when they are both third person.*

For instance: in "I will give it to you" "it" is the direct object and "to you" the indirect; "it" is 3rd Person and "to you" 2nd Person, so the indirect "to you" comes first: *je vous le donnerai.*

BUT in "I will give it to him" both "it" and "to him" are in the 3rd Person, so the direct object comes first: *je le lui donnerai.*

Whether the sentence is in the form of a question or has a "not" in it makes no difference: indirect before direct unless both are in the 3rd Person. Here are further examples:

He has sent it to us. *Il nous l'a envoyé.*
I have sent it to them. *Je le leur ai envoyé.*
Did you give it to him? *Le lui avez-vous donné?*
Didn't he give it to you? *Ne vous l'a-t-il pas donné?*

This last one looks a bit difficult, but it isn't really. The list in Lesson Twelve will give you the pronouns, if you're not sure of them, and the rule just given will tell you the order to put them in. Of course *me* and *nous* are in the 1st Person, *vous* is in the 2nd, and *le, la, les, lui* and *leur* are all in the 3rd Person.

Word List 26

un timbre-poste, (postage) stamp
des timbres-poste, (postage) stamps
la tasse, cup
descendre, to go down, descend, to stay (at a hotel)
rendre, to render, give back

Exercise 26 (a)

Put into English:

1. Pendant que je descendais l'escalier j'ai rencontré un touriste américain qui montait au quatrième étage. 2. Cette vieille femme vendait des fruits et des légumes au marché. 3. Ce vieux monsieur est très pauvre: si vous ne désirez pas

acheter ma vieille bicyclette je la lui donnerai. 4. Mon ami
ne vous prêtera pas sa voiture, parce qu'il me l'a vendue.
5. Ce monsieur est très fâché parce qu'il m'a prêté hier sa
valise et je ne la lui ai pas rendue. 6. Si vous ne me rendez
pas l'argent que vous avez volé les agents de police vous
arrêteront. 7. J'ai écrit une longue lettre à ma cousine,
mais je ne la lui ai pas envoyée. 8. Pourquoi? Parce que je
n'avais pas de timbres-poste. 9. Je vous prêterai un franc
pour acheter des timbres-poste, si vous me le rendez cet
après-midi. 10. Si vous descendez dans la cave vous trouverez des bouteilles de vin rouge qui est très bon. 11. Qui
vous les a données? C'est mon frère qui me les a données. Il
les a reçues d'un ami. 12. Si je n'avais pas vendu ma voiture
je vous l'aurais prêtée.

Exercise 26 (b)

Put into French:

1. I give him some money. 2. He sells me some stamps.
3. I give them to him. 4. He sells them to me. 5. I will give
it (*masc.*) to you. 6. We will give it (*fem.*) to her. 7. I will
show them to you. 8. We used to sell it (*fem.*) to them.
9. He has lent it (*masc.*) to us. 10. He has lent it (*fem.*) to
you. 11. I have not sent it (*masc.*) to her. 12. I have not
sent it (*fem.*) to them.

Exercise 26 (c)

Put into French:

1. If you go down to the dining-room you will find some
cups on the table. 2. I have lent him some money, but he has
not given it back to me. 3. Why has he not given it back to
you? 4. Someone has sold me some very good stamps.
5. I have an old bicycle. I shall lend it to you. 6. I shall not
lend it (*fem.*) to him. 7. Why will you not lend it (*fem.*) to
us? 8. If I had known that you had read this book I would
not have sent it to you. 9. They would have sent it to us.
10. Has he not given them (*masc. pl.*) back to you?

Have a Try 26

Un jour un fermier normand est allé visiter son voisin qui était marchand de charbon (*coal*). "Je suis venu vous demander un petit service," lui dit-il. "Quel service?" "C'est une question du charbon que je désire acheter." "Oui. Dans ces sacs-là il y a du charbon qui est très bon. Si par (*for*) exemple vous désirez dix sacs je vous les vends à dix francs le sac." "C'est assez cher," lui répond le fermier. "Le petit service duquel j'ai parlé, c'est que vous me vendez ce charbon à un prix réduit (*reduced*), parce que je suis un de vos meilleurs amis." "Vous me demandez quelque-chose d'exceptionnel," répond le marchand, "mais puisque (*since*) vous êtes mon ami je vous vends ce charbon à huit francs."

Le fermier est parti très content, mais un mois après il est revenu. "Ce charbon brûle (*burns*) très vite," dit-il. "Je parle du charbon que vous m'avez vendu à un prix réduit parce que je suis un de vos amis." "Ah oui, j'ai réduit le prix du charbon parce que vous êtes un de mes amis, mais parce que je suis un de vos amis j'ai réduit aussi la quantité de charbon que j'ai mis dans les sacs!"

LESSON TWENTY-SEVEN

HOW TO SAY "I BUILD"

The Infinitive of most verbs ends, as we know, in *-er*. In the previous lesson we saw that there are some which end in *-re*. There are also a few with an Infinitive in—*ir*. Such are *bâtir* (to build) and *finir* to (finish).

HERE is the Present Tense of *bâtir*:

je bâtis, I build	*nous bâtissons*
(tu bâtis)	*vous bâtissez*
il bâtit	*ils bâtissent*

All Present Participles end in *-ant*, and we can form the Imperfect Tense by dropping the *-ant* and adding *-ais, -ait* and so on.

Now, the Present Participle of *bâtir* is NOT *bâtant* but *bâtiss-ant*. So the Imperfect is:

je bâtissais, I was building	*nous bâtissions*
(tu bâtissais)	*vous bâtissiez*
il bâtissait	*ils bâtissaient*

The Past Participle is *bâti*: *j'ai bâti*, I (have) built.

How to Change, for Instance, the French for "Sad" into "Sadly"

We know that words such as "sad" or "happy" are adjectives. The words "sadly" and "happily" are known in English as adverbs. Such words usually have the effect of telling us how or in what way something is done. "He walks" simply describes an action. But "he walks slowly" (or "rapidly") tells us how or in what way the person walks. In English an adverb is usually formed by adding "-ly" to the adjective: "quick(ly)", "cheerful(ly)" and so on. In French adverbs are usually formed by adding *-ment* to the FEMININE of the adjective:

110

triste—triste (fem.), sad; *tristement*, sadly
heureux—heureuse (fem.), happy; *heureusement*, happily, fortunately
lent—lente (fem.), slow; *lentement*, slowly
rapide—rapide (fem.), quick, rapid; *rapidement*, quickly, rapidly

Not all adverbs in French are formed in quite this way, but this is the general rule. HERE is one exception to it:

bon, good   *bien*, well

Word List 27

finir, to finish   *choisir*, to choose
fini (Past Participle), finished   *choisi* (Past Participle), chosen
punir, to punish

Exercise 27 (*a*)

Put into English:

1. Les hommes qui bâtissaient une maison dans notre rue, ne travaillent pas aujourd'hui. 2. Si vous ne finissez pas votre travail, vous serez puni. 3. En regardant par ma fenêtre j'ai vu une vieille femme qui marchait très lentement. 4. De ces deux livres lequel choisissez-vous? 5. Hier Mme Dupont choisissait un cadeau pour sa petite fille. Elle est restée longtemps au magasin. 6. J'avais prêté ma bicyclette à mon voisin. Heureusement il me l'a rendue ce matin. 7. Les maisons qui sont bâties de briques sont meilleures que celles qui sont faites de bois. 8. Je finissais mon travail quand elle est entrée dans ma chambre. 9. Vous travaillez très lentement. Les autres ont fini déjà leur travail. 10. Le père de Jean ne le punissait jamais quand il était jeune; maintenant c'est un très méchant homme que les agents de police ont arrêté hier. 11. Quand nous étions jeunes nous choisissions toujours le chocolat au petit déjeuner; aujourd'hui nous préférons le café. 12. Je n'aime pas beaucoup cette maison que ces hommes bâtissent: elle est moins jolie que celle de notre voisin.

Exercise 27 (*b*)

Put into French:

1. I was choosing some postcards in a shop near the church. 2. I am sure that he will work well if you do not punish him. 3. Our neighbour has bought the house which they are building. 4. There are some people who walk very slowly. 5. I went up to his room on the fifth floor, but he was finishing his work. 6. Some bricks have fallen from the house which he was building. 7. Fortunately I have found the knife which I had lost. 8. The person who had taken it had not given it back to me. 9. Do not punish that young man. Why? He is a thief. 10. Those postcards which you were choosing are not very pretty. 11. I was looking for an ugly card. It is for my brother. 12. I have bought you some stamps. Which (ones) do you choose?

Have a Try 27

Les clients qui descendent à l'Hôtel Splendide sont, en général, très riches. Les personnes, qui n'ont pas beaucoup d'argent, choisissent des hôtels plus modestes.

M. Dupuy, qui était énormément riche, mais d'un caractère peu aimable, descendait toujours au Splendide quand il désirait passer deux ou trois jours à Paris.

Un matin au moment où il descendait de sa chambre il y a une panne (*break-down*) d'électricité. En conséquence l'ascenseur est resté immobile. M. Dupuy, très furieux, a fait de grands efforts pour ouvrir (*to open*) la porte de l'ascenseur, mais sans succès. Il est prisonnier.

A cet instant le petit fils d'une des femmes de chambre (*hotel maids*) montait l'escalier. Il avait été au marché où sa mère l'avait envoyé pour acheter des légumes. Ce petit garçon n'aimait pas M. Dupuy, qui était un homme détestable. Il n'a pas fait (*paid*) d'attention aux cris du prisonnier.

Il regarde un instant le captif et, choisissant une grande carotte, il la lui offre.

"Méchant animal," dit-il. "Je vous trouve dans une cage. Aimez-vous les carottes?"

LESSON TWENTY-EIGHT

HOW TO SAY "I SHALL BUILD" AND "I SHALL SELL"

We know (Lesson Twelve) that the Future of *donner* is formed by adding *-ai, -as, -a, -ons, -ez, -ont* to the Infinitive: *je donnerai* and so on. All Future tenses have these same endings. So with *bâtir* we do exactly the same. When the Infinitive of the verb ends in *-re* we drop the *e* before adding the endings. So we have:

je bâtirai, I shall build	*je vendrai*, I shall sell
(tu bâtiras)	*(tu vendras)*
il bâtira	*il vendra*
nous bâtirons	*nous vendrons*
vous bâtirez	*vous vendrez*
ils bâtiront	*ils vendront*

Now, as we know, the Conditional ("I should") of *donner* is formed by adding to it the endings *-ais, -ais, -ait, -ions, -iez, -aient*. All Conditionals have these same endings. So we can add them to the Infinitive *bâtir*, and to *vendre*, though here again we drop the final *e*.

je bâtirais, I should build	*je vendrais*, I should sell
(tu bâtirais)	*(tu vendrais)*
il bâtirait	*il vendrait*
nous bâtirions	*nous vendrions*
vous bâtiriez	*vous vendriez*
ils bâtiraient	*ils vendraient*

How to Say "Who?" and "Whom?"

We have already used *qui* with the meaning of "who", "which" and *que* with the meaning of "whom", "which", *qui* being the subject pronoun and *que* the object pronoun.

l'homme qui est à la porte, the man who is at the door
l'homme que j'ai vu, the man whom I saw
les vaches qui sont dans le champ, the cows which are in the field
les choses que vous achetez, the things which you buy.

114

qui and *que* as used in the above sentences are what are called relative pronouns. BUT we often use "who" and "which" to ask questions, that is as interrogative pronouns.

COMPARE these two:

The boy who is with you is the tallest in the school. *Le garçon qui est avec vous est le plus grand de l'école.*
Who is that tall boy? *Qui est ce grand garçon?*

The first *qui* is a relative pronoun, the second *qui* is an interrogative pronoun.

As subject of the verb *est* we use *qui* in both sentences.

NOW compare these two:

the boy whom I saw, *le garçon que j'ai vu*
Whom did you see? *Qui avez-vous vu?*

So in RELATIVE sentences we use *qui* as subject and *que* as object. BUT in interrogative sentences *qui?* is used for both "who?" and "whom?". In both kinds of sentence *qui* is used after prepositions such as *à* and *de*.

le garçon de qui je parle, the boy of whom I am speaking
A qui (de qui) parlez-vous? To whom (of whom) are you speaking?

The relative *qui* and *que* can be used of people or of things.

l'homme qui est là, the man who was there
l'arbre qui est tombé, the tree which has fallen
la maison que je bâtis, the house which I build
le soldat que j'ai rencontré, the soldier whom I (have) met

BUT *qui?* interrogative means only "who?" or "whom?". It can be used only of people, not of things. So how are we to say "What have you done?" or "What has happened?"? "What?" as object of a verb is *que?* (or, before a vowel *qu'*). So "What have you done?" is *Qu-avez-vous fait?*

BUT with "what?" as subject of the verb we have to use *qu'est-ce qui?* (this is really "what is it which?").

What has happened? *Qu'est-ce qui est arrivé?*
Who has arrived? *Qui est arrivé?*
Whom have you seen? *Qui avez-vous vu?*
What are you looking for? *Que cherchez-vous?*

In fact, it is only "what?" as subject of a sentence, *qu'est-ce qui?* which is difficult.

Word List 28

entendre, to hear   *le bruit*, noise
attendre, to wait *or* to wait for

Exercise 28 (*a*)

Put into English:

1. Qui est ce monsieur qui a bâti cette maison? C'est un médecin. 2. Il m'a dit qu'il me vendrait son couteau, mais il l'a perdu. 3. Quel est ce bruit que j'ai entendu? Qu'avez-vous fait? 4. Je jetais des briques. Vous trouverez que la fenêtre de la salle à manger est cassée. 5. Qui est cette dame et que lui avez-vous dit? 6. Qui attendiez-vous quand je vous ai vu ce matin dans la place du marché? 7. Si elle n'est pas à la gare à six heures et demie, je ne l'attendrai pas. 8. Il y a une foule de personnes devant l'église: qu'est-ce qui arrive? 9. Je le punirais s'il était plus intelligent. Il travaille bien mais c'est le garçon le plus bête de la classe. 10. Qui cherchez-vous? Ma cousine. Elle m'a dit qu'elle serait ici à midi, mais elle n'est pas arrivée. 11. Que désirez-vous acheter? Des légumes et du fromage. 12. Qui vous a dit que le train de deux heures ne s'arrête pas ici? 13. Qu'est-ce qui arrivera s'il tombe dans cette eau profonde?

Exercise 28 (*b*)

Put into French:

1. Whom are you waiting for? 2. We are waiting for him. 3. What have you heard? 4. I heard the noise of the men who are cutting the trees. 5. What has he done? He has stolen some money. 6. Who are those people to whom you were speaking? 7. I am not sure when he will build his house. 8. I will sell you some wine. 9. If she does not walk quickly I shall not wait for her. 10. What will happen if the train has already departed? 11. What will you sell? 12. What did she say to you? 13. Who told you that the

train will not stop here? 14. There are always some free
seats (places) in the trains which stop here. 15. Who is that
young man whom the police have arrested? He is the
farmer's son. 16. They made so much noise that the landlord heard them. 17. These vegetables are very good. Will
you sell them to me? 18. Whom did you meet this morning?
19. Do you hear those birds? I do not hear them. 20. You
would hear them, if there was less noise.

Have a Try 28

Mme Lebrun et les deux garçons attendaient l'arrivée de
l'autobus dans lequel ils allaient monter pour retourner à
Dieppe. Parmi la foule il y avait un homme qui, s'appro-
chant avec précaution d'une dame, a pris le grand paquet
qu'elle portait sous le bras (arm).

"C'est un voleur!" cria Jean. "Allons le chercher!"
"Mais non," dit la dame qui, à la surprise de ses compagnons
de voyage, n'a pas l'air d'être fâchée. "Mais nous aurions
fait notre possible pour l'attraper, madame," dit Jean.
"Merci," répond la dame, "mais ce sera le voleur qui ne sera
pas content. Mon pauvre petit chat, qui était très vieux, est
mort (died) hier. J'occupe un appartement en ville, mais j'ai
une amie qui a un joli jardin. Elle a promis d'enterrer
(bury) mon chat et c'est ce pauvre petit animal que le voleur
trouvera dans le paquet qu'il a pris!"

LESSON TWENTY-NINE

MORE ABOUT NUMBERS

So far we know the numbers up to 61—*soixante et un*; 69 would therefore be *soixante-neuf*.

When we come to 70, however, we have to put *soixante-dix* (60-10), so that 71 is 60-11—*soixante et onze*.

When we come to 80 we reckon this as 4 times 20 and put *quatre-vingts*. There is no need to list every number, but the following list should be helpful:

60, *soixante*	90, *quatre-vingt-dix*
61, *soixante et un*	91, *quatre-vingt-onze*
62, *soixante-deux*	94, *quatre-vingt-quatorze*
69, *soixante-neuf*	99, *quatre-vingt-dix-neuf*
70, *soixante-dix*	100, *cent*
71, *soixante et onze*	101, *cent un*
72, *soixante-douze*	102, *cent deux*
78, *soixante-dix-huit*	200, *deux cents*
79, *soixante-dix-neuf*	201, *deux cent un*
80, *quatre-vingts*	1000, *mille* (in dates *mil*)
81, *quatre-vingt-un*	2000, *deux mille* (*deux milles* = 2 miles)
89, *quatre-vingt-neuf*	

TRY to REMEMBER that:

(1) There is an *et* in 21 up to 71 but not in 81, 91 or usually, in 101.

(2) That there is an *s* on *quatre-vingts* (80) and on 200, 300 and so on: *deux cents, trois cents*, but only when the number is exactly 80 or an exact 200 or 300: in other words no *s* on 81 or on 201.

(3) When there is no *et* there is a dash - in all numbers between 17 and 99.

In 153, for instance, we put *cent cinquante-trois*, putting the dash - only between that part of the number which comes between the limits of 17 and 99, in this case 53.

IN DATES we do not translate the English "and" unless, of course, there is already an *et* in the French number.

So 1964, *mil neuf cent soixante-quatre.* BUT 1921, *mil neuf cent vingt et un.*

WHEN talking about kings and queens we say "Henry the eighth". In French there is no *le* and save for "1st" (*premier*), the ordinary numbers *deux, trois* are used (as in dates of the month).

Charles the First (Charles I), *Charles premier*
Charles the Ninth (Charles IX), *Charles neuf*

The use of *en*

So FAR we have used *en* only as a preposition meaning "in": *en France*; *en silence.* In most cases we are more likely to use *dans*: *dans la ville.*

BUT *en* is also a pronoun and may mean "of it", "of them", "some", "from it", "from them". Like the object pronouns *me, le* and the rest, *en* comes in front of the verb.

IN ENGLISH, in answer to the question "Have you any money?" we may reply "Yes, I have" or "Yes, I have some" or (more likely) "No, I haven't (any)."

In French this "some" or "any" must be put in.

Avez-vous de l'argent? Oui, j'en ai or *J'en ai beaucoup* (I have a lot of it) or *Non, je n'en ai pas.*

IF there is another object pronoun *en* always comes second of the two. For instance, in reply to the question about money we might (rashly!) say:

Yes, I will lend you some. *Oui, je vous en prêterai.*

Word List 29

régner, to reign
un accident, accident
la vitesse, speed (*also* gear)

la collection, collection
un an, a year

Exercise 29 (*a*)

Put into English:

1. Dans ce grand avion il y a des places pour cent vingt-cinq personnes. 2. Cet avion a volé de Paris à New York en huit heures et demie—une distance de trois mille milles ou

quatre mille huit cents kilomètres. 3. J'ai perdu votre couteau: heureusement j'en ai un autre que je vous donnerai. 4. Le roi Louis quatorze a régné pendant soixante-douze ans. 5. Il a été roi de France de mil six cent quarante-trois jusqu'à mil sept cent quinze. 6. Nous n'avons pas d'argent mais ma sœur vous en prêtera. 7. Etes-vous sûr qu'elle nous attendra? Oui, j'en suis sûr, elle me l'a dit deux fois. 8. Cette voiture qui a blessé un petit garçon pendant qu'il traversait la rue allait trop vite. 9. Oui. Beaucoup trop vite. Elle allait à une vitesse de cent cinq kilomètres à l'heure. 10. Combien de maisons y a-t-il dans la rue où vous demeurez? Il y en a quatre-vingt-douze. 11. Avez-vous beaucoup de timbres-poste dans votre collection? J'en ai quinze cents. 12. Mon oncle qui a beaucoup voyagé m'a envoyé des timbres-poste. Je vous en donnerai une douzaine des meilleurs. 13. Merci beaucoup. Vous êtes très aimable. J'ai des livres français que je vous prêterai, si vous n'en avez pas. J'en ai deux ou trois qui sont très intéressants. 14. Qui est cet auteur que nous avons rencontré au café? C'est Monsieur Vite. Il a écrit cent trente-trois livres. Je lui ai dit que j'en avais lu deux!

Exercise 29 (b)

Put into French:

1. An accident has happened to the train. Three travellers have been killed and there are sixty-five (of them) who are wounded. 2. Queen Victoria (has) reigned for (during) sixty-four years. 3. She was the Queen of England from 1837 (in words) until 1901 (in words). 4. We haven't any double rooms on the first floor, madam; but there are two (of them) on the third floor. 5. They (refers to "rooms") will be free this afternoon. Are you sure? Yes, I am sure. 6. I would not have bought these newspapers if I had known that you have three already. 7. The motor-car into which we had got (*monter*) was going at 85 kilometres per (to the) hour. 8. Did you hear that noise during the night? Yes, I

was speaking of it to the landlord. 9. I have finished my letter, but I have no stamps. Have you any? 10. Yes. I bought a dozen (of them) at the café this morning. I will lend you two or three (of them). 11. Marseilles is at a distance of 800 kilometres from Paris. 12. I went to Paris for the first time in (*en* not *dans*) 1961 (in words).

Have a Try 29
News Items

1. Le Gouvernement examinera les circonstances de la catastrophe du train Calais–Paris qui a déraillé à l'entrée de la gare d'Abbeville. Cet accident a coûté la vie au mécanicien et à treize voyageurs et cent personnes ont été blessées.

2. A Los Angeles l'équipe d'Angleterre de football a battu celle des Etats Unis par 8 buts à 1. L'equipe du Real Madrid est partie pour Stuttgart où elle rencontrera celle de Reims (*Rheims*) en finale de la Coupe d'Europe de football.

3. Ce mois (*month*) marque une date de victoire pour la télévision. La première émission de télévision destinée simultanément à plusieurs (*several*) pays a eu lieu (*took place*) en 1954. Pendant sept jours dix-neuf programmes ont été retransmis et le Pape (*Pope*) a parlé dans leur langue nationale aux spectateurs de huit pays. L'Eurovision, qui avait transmis en 1953 le couronnement de la Reine d'Angleterre, a cessé (*ceased*) d'être un miracle.

(Adapted from *Le Figaro*)

LESSON THIRTY

HOW TO SAY "I HAVE HIDDEN MYSELF"

We saw in Lesson Twenty-five how to use verbs like *se cacher* when the subject and object of the verb refer to the same person (or thing).

We hide ourselves. *Nous nous cachons.*
He will hide himself. *Il se cachera.*

Now if we want to say "he has hidden himself" we should expect to use *il a*. In fact, however, with these "reflexive" verbs, as they are called, that is ones where the subject and object refer to the same person or thing, we use *il est*. This applies ONLY WHEN THE VERB IS USED REFLEXIVELY THUS:

He has hidden himself in the wood. *Il s'est caché dans les arbres.*

BUT

She has hidden him. *Elle l'a caché* (because the subject and object are two different people).

In Lesson Nineteen we learned the important rule that when a Past Participle has a tense of *avoir* (*a, avait* and so on) with it the participle agrees with its direct object, provided that this direct object comes BEFORE it. Now, with these reflexive verbs, although we are using *est* not *a*, the meaning is "has" not "is", and here, too, the Past Participle agrees with the direct object pronoun in front of it.

Tuer, to kill. So,

He has killed them. *Il les a tués.*

And

She (has) killed herself. *Elle s'est tuée.*

SIMILARLY with other tenses:

He would have killed her. *Il l'aurait tuée.*
She would have killed herself. *Elle se serait tuée.*

122

The Meaning of *on*

In English we sometimes use the word "one", not as a number, but in the more general sense of "people", "someone" or "they" not referring to anyone in particular. The French use *on* (third person singular) in the same way.

someone told me *or* I have been told, *on m'a dit*
French is spoken here (*notice in a shop window*). *Ici on parle français.*
One often finds rabbits in this field. *On trouve souvent des lapins dans ce champ.*

Word List 30

vrai, true	*quelquefois*, sometimes
un morceau, a bit, a piece	*un siècle*, century
la tête, head	

Exercise 30 (*a*)

Put into English:

1. La pauvre petite fille s'est tuée en tombant dans l'eau. 2. Si elle était tombée dans l'eau elle se serait tuée. 3. On m'a dit que vous alliez vendre votre maison. Est-ce vrai? 4. Je cherche mes deux frères. Les avez-vous vus? Où se sont-ils cachés? 5. Nous nous sommes habillés vite, parce que nous allions au bord de la mer. 6. On entend souvent des bruits dans ce bois pendant la nuit. 7. Pendant le seizième siècle on a bâti en France de très beaux châteaux. 8. Pourquoi êtes-vous entré dans ce petit magasin? Je cherchais de vieux livres. On en trouve quelquefois dans ces petits magasins. 9. Si vous vous étiez cachés dans le bois, on ne vous aurait pas trouvés. 10. Il est vrai qu'on a entendu quelqu'un qui entrait dans l'hôtel pendant la nuit. 11. On nous a dit qu'au quinzième siècle un général s'est tué dans une des chambres du palais. 12. Où est l'arbre dans lequel le roi Charles deux s'est caché? Il est tombé et on l'a coupé en morceaux.

Exercise 30 (*b*)

Put into French:

1. One often meets people (use *personne*) who have been to Paris. 2. Is it true that she has won the first prize? People have told me so (*le*). 3. The motor-car did not stop. The police have arrested the owner (of it). 4. We were looking for the boys, but they had hidden themselves. 5. Someone has shut the door and I haven't the key (of it). 6. The thieves wounded themselves in (*en*) entering the house by the window. 7. This bottle did not break itself! It is he who broke it. 8. The big book, which he had thrown out of (*par*)

the window, fell on the head of a policeman. 9. That poor old woman has thrown herself on the (railway) track in front of a train which was approaching. 10. Fortunately the train stopped, because it was going at a speed of 25 kilometres an (to the) hour. 11. During the eighteenth century, if you had taken a sheep or something which was not yours (to you) they (not *ils*) would have killed you. 12. She dressed herself very quickly, because she was going to meet her friends at half past seven.

Have a Try 30

"Vous rappelez-vous (*recall, remember*) la famille française que nous avons rencontrée quand nous voyagions en

Normandie?" "Oui, très bien. Il y avait le père, la mère et
deux enfants." "Oui, c'est exact. Ils avaient pris déjà leurs
places quand nous sommes montés dans le train à Rouen et
j'ai pensé au commencement que j'allais les détester!"
"Moi, aussi. Le temps était beau mais la dame a insisté que
les fenêtres restent fermées." "Oui, mais c'était une dame
très aimable." "C'est vrai. Nous n'avions pas assez d'argent
pour aller déjeuner au wagon-restaurant." "Non, nous
avions acheté à la gare un petit paquet de chocolat."
"Oui. Et cette dame admirable, qui avait apporté du pain,
du jambon (*ham*) et des fruits pour le repas de la famille nous
a invités à en manger." "Et nous avons refusé—par polit-
esse! Heureusement elle a insisté!" "Oui, j'ai noté tous ces
détails dans mon journal (here 'diary', note-book) du
voyage."

LESSON THIRTY-ONE

HOW TO SAY "MINE" AND "OURS"

We know already how to use *mon, ma* and the rest. They are always used with nouns: *mon père, sa tante.*

In a sentence such as "this dog is mine" we don't want to have to say *ce chien est mon chien,* we want to know the French for "mine" to save repeating the word *chien.*

The following table will show us how to do this:

Masc. Sing.	Fem. Sing.	Masc. Pl.	Fem. Pl.	Eng.
le mien	*la mienne*	*les miens*	*les miennes*	mine
(le tien)	*(la tienne)*	*(les tiens)*	*(les tiennes)*	(thine)
le sien	*la sienne*	*les siens*	*les siennes*	his, hers
le nôtre	*la nôtre*	*les nôtres*	*les nôtres*	ours
le vôtre	*la vôtre*	*les vôtres*	*les vôtres*	yours
le leur	*la leur*	*les leurs*	*les leurs*	theirs

REMEMBER that *son* and *sa* can each mean either "his" or "her" because we have to go by the gender of the noun and not by the sex of the owner, so *son père* can be either "his father" or "her father", and *sa mère*, "her mother" or "his mother". In the same way *le sien* and *la sienne* can each mean either "his" or "hers". Which we put depends on the gender of the noun to which the possessive refers.

Our house is smaller than his (hers). *Notre maison est plus petite que la sienne.*

REMEMBER that although the plural of *notre* and *votre* is *nos, vos, le nôtre* and *le vôtre* merely add "s" to the singular *les nôtres, les vôtres.*

How to Say "I am right (wrong)"

There are some phrases where in English we use "to be" but the French use *avoir.*

For instance, "How old are you?" becomes in French "What age have you?"—*Quel âge avez-vous?* So the answer

is NOT *Je suis onze ans*, BUT, say, *J'ai onze ans* (I am eleven).
  OTHER such expressions are:

to be right, *avoir raison*   to be sea-sick, *avoir le mal de mer*
to be wrong, *avoir tort*   to be in need of (to need), *avoir besoin de*

Word List 31

encore, still, yet   *le porte-monnaie*, purse

Exercise 31 (*a*)

Put into English:

1. Votre sœur n'est pas très grande. Quel âge a-t-elle?
Elle a quinze ans. 2. J'avais dix ans quand je suis allé pour
la première fois au bord de la mer. 3. Notre maison est
plus petite que la vôtre, mais nous préférons la nôtre parce
qu'elle a un très joli jardin. 4. Ma voiture est celle-ci: la
leur est devant l'hôtel. 5. Elle a perdu son porte-monnaie,
mais j'ai trouvé le mien. On l'avait mis sur cette table.
6. Vous avez raison: c'est lui qui a tort. 7. Si vous n'aviez
pas mangé tant de pommes vertes vous n'auriez pas le mal
de mer. 8. Vous aurez besoin de tout votre argent pour
acheter cette collection de timbres-poste. 9. Nous avons
trouvé notre chien, mais mon amie cherche le sien. 10. Où
est votre méchant petit neveu? Il n'est jamais là quand on a
besoin de lui. 11. Vos livres sont plus intéressants que les
nôtres, mais les siens sont encore meilleurs. 12. Votre tante
et la mienne ont quarante ans, mais mon oncle est plus
vieux que le vôtre.

Exercise 31 (*b*)

Put into French:

1. I am eight years old. (On) Thursday my father will be
thirty-nine years old. 2. How old was she when she came to
spend her holidays with you? She was seventeen years old.
3. Louis XIV was five years old when he became King of
France. 4. There are more sheep in our field than in hers.

5. There are more flowers in our room than in his. 6. You told me that he was fourteen years old, but you were wrong. 7. If you do not need those shoes, will you give them to me? 8. He told me that my brother and his had gone to the cinema. Was he right? 9. The room into which the gentleman went is not his: they gave him a room on the second floor. 10. How old is your dog? On Sunday he will be fourteen. And yours? Oh, he is still young. 11. I had lost my suitcase, but they have lent me theirs, which is bigger than mine. 12. I will give you my shoes. I shall not have need of them, because they have become too small.

Have a Try 31

L'heure du départ est arrivée. "Vous avez été bien aimable. Merci mille fois," dit Charles à Mme Lebrun et à Jean qui l'ont accompagné jusqu'au bureau de la Compagnie "Air France".

Une employée de la Compagnie s'approche d'un haut parleur et annonce, "Les passagers par Air France à destination de Londres sont priés de monter dans l'autobus."

A onze heures Charles et ses compagnons de voyage descendent de l'autobus à l'aéroport d'Orly. Le trajet (*trip*) dans le grand avion—c'est une "Caravelle" avec des places pour quatre-vingt quinze passagers—dure très peu de temps. En réponse aux questions d'un douanier (*customs officer*) Charles déclare qu'il n'y a pas de cigares dans sa valise, et qu'il n'a pas de montres cachées dans ses poches (*pockets*).

A la barrière il trouve sa mère qui est venue le rencontrer.

"Je suis sûre que vous vous êtes bien amusé en France," lui dit-elle. "Parlez-vous bien le français maintenant?"

"Mais non," répond Charles. "Mais j'ai fait de grands progrès."

(The author hopes that this may also be true of those who have worked through this book.)

PART II

KEY TO EXERCISES

Exercise 1 (*a*)

1. The boy is in the garden. 2. The actress is at the door of the house. 3. Where is the soldier? He is at the hotel. 4. Where is the woman? She is at the church. 5. The boys are in the street. 6. A cow and a sheep are in the garden behind the house. 7. The man who is at the hotel is an officer. 8. Where are the cows? They are in the field behind the church. 9. The actress who is in the street is the wife of the officer. 10. A soldier is at the door of the hotel with a woman who is the daughter of an actress.

Exercise 1 (*b*)

1. Le garçon est derrière un arbre dans le jardin. 2. L'officier est avec les soldats dans la rue. 3. Où sont les filles? Elles sont dans la maison. 4. Où sont les moutons? Ils sont dans le champ derrière l'hôtel. 5. Les filles de l'actrice sont dans l'église. 6. Le garçon est à la porte de l'hôtel. 7. La femme de l'officier est dans la rue. 8. Où sont les soldats? Ils sont dans le champ avec l'officier. 9. Une vache et un mouton sont dans le jardin. 10. La femme qui est à la porte de l'église est la fille de l'actrice. 11. L'homme et la femme sont dans les champs. 12. Où est la vache? Elle est dans le jardin.

Have a Try 1

The lion is a dangerous animal. In the Zoological Garden(s) in Paris and in London he (it) is in a cage. The spectator is behind a barrier. The hippopotamus—an extraordinary creature—is content, but for the tiger and the leopard captivity is, perhaps, cruel.

Exercise 2 (*a*)

1. The car is old, but it is good. 2. The little daughter of the actress is in the garden with two (boy) friends. 3. The books which are on the table in the room of the old woman are very good. 4. The three daughters of the queen are in a fine car in front of the big church. 5. The room where we are is very high. 6. Where are the two little (girl) cousins of the officer? They are in the field behind the hotel. 7. I am in front of the door of the house with two friends. 8. We are in a pretty house which is very old. 9. The trees in the field where the two little sheep are, are very tall. 10. Where is the cow? In the field? It is on the bed in the room of the old woman (the old woman's room).

Exercise 2 (*b*)

1. Nous sommes à un joli hôtel dans la ville. 2. L'hôtel est vieux, mais les chambres sont bonnes. 3. La rue devant la maison où nous sommes est longue. 4. Où sont les moutons? Ils sont derrière les grands arbres dans le champ. 5. Deux hommes, trois petits garçons et une vieille femme sont dans la voiture. 6. Les deux petites cousines de l'actrice sont ici. La maison où elles sont est belle. 7. Les lits dans les chambres à l'hôtel sont très petits. 8. La fille de l'officier et un ami sont dans la rue derrière la vieille église. 9. Les livres qui sont sur la petite table derrière la porte sont bons. 10. Les maisons dans la rue sont petites, mais elles sont belles.

Have a Try 2

It is evident that the cows and the sheep are stupid, but I am certain that the elephant is a very intelligent animal. In a

zoo and in a circus he is gentle, but it is preferable to observe
(the) elephants in the excellent colour films in which (where)
the wild beasts are at liberty among the rivers, the forests
and the plains of Africa or India.

Exercise 3 (*a*)

1. Have you a present for the little son of the farmer's
wife? 2. No. He is very naughty. When the other boys are
at (the) school he is in the wood. 3. The two big cars which
are in front of the hotel belong to the officer: he is very rich.
4. Where are the two sons of the young actress? 5. They are
on the river in a boat: the water is very deep. 6. The actress
who is at the hotel with two friends has a beautiful voice.
7. Where is the Queen's palace? She has a palace in London
and a castle at Windsor. 8. Where are the newspapers? They
are on the little table. 9. The two horses and the old cows
which are in the field between the street and the river belong
to the farmer's wife. 10. We are sure that the presents in the
room of the actress are for us.

Exercise 3 (*b*)

1. La grande maison qui est dans le champ derrière
l'hôtel est à la reine. 2. Etes-vous sûr qu'elle est ici? Oui.
Elle est à l'église. 3. Les deux soldats qui sont dans la rue
ont une petite voiture, mais le beau cheval dans le champ est
à l'officier. 4. Nous sommes sûrs que les vieilles vaches et les
trois moutons sont à la fermière. 5. Sont-ils à l'école?
Non. Ils sont dans les bois. 6. Les chambres dans le château
sont très grandes. 7. Les fils de l'actrice sont sur le fleuve
avec les autres garçons. 8. Elle est sûre que les cadeaux sont
pour vous. 9. Les journaux sont à nous, mais le livre est à
vous. 10. Où est la pauvre vieille femme? Est-elle ici?
Non. Elle est dans la ville avec le fermier.

Have a Try 3

At the door of a palace in Paris three officers get out of a car. The big house belongs to a very important person, the President of the Republic. The soldiers who are in front of the main door are in the uniform of the republican guard. The three visitors are very distinguished: the first is a general, the second is an admiral and the third is a marshal of the Air Force. In (the) battles with the enemies of France they have been very brave, and they are invited to the presidential house (the president's house) to receive the medals which are the reward of an exceptional courage.

Exercise 4 (a)

1. We have spent two days in Paris with a friend. 2. The farmer's wife is very cross because the naughty little boy has stolen the meat. 3. An old actress has bought the fine house where we have spent the holidays. 4. We have spoken to the man who has bought the horses. 5. They have travelled to the town to look for a friend. 6. Have you found the newspapers? No, but I am sure that they are here. 7. The men who have worked in the fields yesterday are in the woods. 8. The soldiers have marched to the town. 9. A wicked man has stolen the money of the poor woman (the poor woman's money). 10. The little girl to whom I have spoken yesterday has spent the holidays in London.

Exercise 4 (b)

1. Où avez-vous caché l'argent? Derrière un arbre dans le jardin. 2. Ils ont acheté un bateau pour passer les vacances avec un ami. 3. Nous avons voyagé à Paris pour regarder les magasins. 4. Avez-vous cherché le pauvre vieux chien? 5. Oui. Il est avec deux autres chiens dans le champ derrière l'église. 6. J'ai parlé à l'homme qui a acheté l'hôtel. 7. Nous sommes sûrs qu'elle a passé trois jours à Paris.

8. Ils ont cherché dans la maison et dans le jardin, mais ont-ils trouvé l'argent? 9. Avez-vous acheté le journal? Non, mais nous avons acheté deux livres. 10. Hier nous avons marché à la ville pour acheter un cadeau pour un ami.

Have a Try 4

The Prince of X, who is the owner of a big castle in Italy, has a very fine collection of pictures, of rare books and other precious objects. Yesterday a criminal armed with a revolver (has) penetrated into the great gallery of the huge house with the intention of stealing a diamond of enormous value. But a faithful dog has given (gave) the alarm, a servant (has) telephoned to the police and two policemen (have) arrested the bandit.

Exercise 5 (a)

1. I have spoken yesterday to the owner of the castle. 2. The water of the river is not very deep. 3. We (have) spent two hours in the garden while the other tourists (have) visited the church near the market. 4. Have you bought today's paper? No. The newspapers are not very interesting. 5. John's mother is very angry because the naughty little boy has stolen the doctor's hat. 6. We have looked everywhere for the little sons of the farmer. 7. Are they ill? No. I am sure that they are not ill. 8. Where have you hidden the two books which belong to John's cousin? I have not hidden the books: they are on the table near the window. 9. Why have you looked (did you look) yesterday for the tourists? They are not here, I am sure that they are in Paris. 10. At the little shop near the market we have bought three books for John's cousin.

Exercise 5 (b)

1. Nous avons parlé de vous au propriétaire de l'hôtel qui est près du marché. 2. Le chien qui est dans le champ

n'est pas à nous, mais au fermier. 3. L'officier et les soldats
ont marché de la ville au palais du roi. 4. Les touristes ont
passé trois jours à Tours pour visiter les vieux châteaux du
pays. 5. Nous avons cherché partout le chien du propriétaire. 6. L'actrice qui est à l'hôtel est très fâchée parce
que le chien a caché deux vieilles bottines dans le lit. 7. La
femme de l'officier a acheté une jolie petite maison. 8. Elle
n'est pas près de la ville, mais elle est près du fleuve. 9. Nous
n'avons pas visité l'église, mais nous avons regardé les
tableaux dans le palais du roi. 10. J'ai parlé aux jeunes fils
du médecin.

Have a Try 5

In a very famous book an author (has) related the adven-
tures of a small boy who (has) found in the baggage of an
old sailor the map of an island where a pirate has hidden a
vast treasure. A very rich man to whom the boy has spoken
of the map decided to travel in search of the treasure. The
journey is not without incident, because the sailors who
(have) accompanied the man and the boy are in reality the
pirate's old companions (shipmates).

Exercise 6 (a)

1. My cousins and the American actress have taken the
train for Bordeaux. 2. Our French friends have bought a
nice white house (at) two kilometres from the town where
we have spent our holidays. 3. Have you made (did you
make) an interesting journey with your father? 4. Yes, we
(have) spent three weeks in a little village near Mont Blanc.
5. The tourist who is the owner of the big black car is
English, but his wife is French. 6. My two Italian friends
and their little sister (have) made yesterday a fine excursion.
7. Who has put the old black cow into my beautiful car?
8. Have you seen my daughter? She is not at (the) school.
9. My sons and their friends are in one of the little boats

which belong to the doctor of our village. 10. My aunt has grey hair, but she is not old.

Exercise 6 (*b*)

1. Où avez-vous mis mes journaux français? Ils ne sont pas sur la table dans ma chambre. 2. Notre médecin et sa vieille mère ont pris le train pour Paris. 3. Vos sœurs ne sont pas ici. Elles sont dans un bateau sur le fleuve avec deux jeunes hommes du village. 4. Les vieilles églises grises dans nos villages sont intéressantes, mais sont-elles belles? 5. Notre médecin et sa tante ont passé leurs vacances à Paris. 6. Ma sœur et son fils ont visité les vieux palais des rois français. 7. La fermière est très fâchée parce que vos moutons sont dans son jardin. 8. Les bottines noires ne sont pas à vous. 9. Nous avons regardé la maison blanche où vous avez passé vos vacances. 10. Nous avons travaillé aujourd'hui avec les deux fils du fermier dans les bois derrière leur maison.

Have a Try 6

The streets in the centre of Paris are, in general, very wide, but when I made my first visit to Paris with two school friends, we found a certain difficulty in crossing the streets because of the great number of cars, taxis and buses which (have) passed, and because the rule of the road is different in France, where it is necessary to keep to the right.

In a shop near our hotel I bought a plan of Paris and we visited the chief public buildings of the town, for instance, the Louvre, a former royal palace, which today is a museum, and the Cathedral of Notre Dame (Our Lady).

Exercise 7 (*a*)

1. Flowers are beautiful, trees are useful. 2. The sons and daughters of the doctor have made an excursion to the

country. 3. Why have you not done your work? 4. Where is your sister? Has she taken the train for Bordeaux with her friends? 5. Who are the little girls to whom you have spoken at (in) the market? 6. They are the cousins of the man who has bought the big white house near the church. 7. Mary's father and mother are the owners of a little shop in the market-place. 8. Why did she not take all her books to school? 9. Elephants are more intelligent than sheep. 10. One of the officers has bought all the white cows which are in the farmer's field.

Exercise 7 (b)

1. Mon père et ma mère ont voyagé dans tous les pays du monde. 2. Le chien est un animal qui est très utile aux hommes. 3. Tous les animaux ne sont pas intelligents. 4. Pourquoi n'a-t-il pas pris l'argent qui est sur la table dans sa chambre? 5. Où avez-vous acheté les vieux livres? J'ai acheté tous les livres dans un petit magasin derrière l'église. 6. Je n'ai pas vu la tante de mon ami parce que nous avons passé toute la semaine à la campagne. 7. La vieille actrice italienne a acheté la voiture grise pour ses fils et pour ses filles. 8. Où a-t-elle caché son argent? 9. Tous les soldats ont marché derrière leur officier au palais. 10. Avez-vous cherché vos livres dans toutes les chambres de la maison?

Have a Try 7

In a Parisian newspaper I found a very amusing story yesterday. Mrs. X is employed as secretary in a big shop near the Seine. She is not rich, but she has a passion for flowers. She has the (a) habit of placing a vase of flowers on the ledge of the balcony. Yesterday by mistake she let her vase fall just at the moment when the owner of the house (firm), a very bad-tempered man, was on the point of entering the shop. The poor man is in hospital, and Mrs. X is obliged to look for another situation.

Exercise 8 (a)

1. In this hotel the meals are very good. 2. The two men who are getting into that car are the brothers of your friend John. 3. Where did you buy these presents? 4. Who lives in this (that) ugly little house? 5. Where are you going? We are going to visit that big castle three kilometres from the village. 6. That little girl is not very intelligent. When she crosses the river she often falls into the water. 7. Why are you looking at that old woman? Who is she? 8. Did you live for a long time in this town? 9. For those women who work in a factory life is often very hard. 10. We are sure that that boy who is getting into that train is the farmer's son.

Exercise 8 (b)

1. Qui est ce jeune homme qui marche vers l'église? 2. Demeurez-vous dans une de ces vieilles maisons qui sont à notre médecin? 3. N'allez-vous pas souvent au cinéma avec votre mère et votre père? 4. Nous demeurons dans la ville, mais ma tante a passé sa vie à la campagne. 5. Nous allons souvent à l'usine dans la voiture de mon père, mais hier nous avons pris le train. 6. Tous les moutons qui traversent la rue sont à ce fermier qui a acheté votre maison. 7. Où avez-vous mis votre argent? Je cache mon argent pendant que je suis à l'école. 8. Nous allons donner au chien la viande qui est sur cette table (-là). 9. Mon frère travaille dans une usine à trois kilomètres de la ville. 10. Allez-vous souvent à Rome? J'ai demeuré longtemps à Rome et j'ai visité toutes les grandes villes italiennes.

Have a Try 8

The tourists get into the bus and after an hour they arrive at the entrance to London airport. There the bus goes down into a long passage which is like a tunnel, and goes up again to the surface. A pretty girl who is an employee of "Air France" guides the travellers to the point of departure. They go into the inside of (they go inside) the big plane. The pilot, navigator and wireless operator have already taken their places. The big jet engines are put into motion (are started up) and the journey by air (the flight) begins.

Exercise 9 (a)

1. Are you looking for something? Yes. I am looking for my books, but I do not find them. 2. Where have you put your exercise-book? I put it on the table in my room. 3. Where is my dog? Have you seen it (him)? No, I haven't seen it. 4. Where are you going to spend your holidays? We always spend them in the country. 5. Why didn't you take the train? I didn't take it because I haven't my ticket. 6. Have you lost it? No. Your naughty little dog ate it. 7. I have looked everywhere for the doctor, but I haven't found him. 8. Who is that man who is looking at us? 9. Your sister is not at school. Hasn't she done her work? 10. Yes. She has done it, but she is at the house today because she is ill.

Exercise 9 (b)

1. Ce chapeau-là n'est pas joli. Où l'avez-vous acheté? 2. Je ne l'ai pas acheté. Je l'ai trouvé dans l'autobus. 3. Je cherche mon frère. Ne l'avez-vous pas vu? 4. Non. Je ne l'ai pas vu, mais je suis sûr qu'il n'est pas ici. 5. La cherchez-vous? Non. Je ne la cherche pas. 6. Où achetez-vous vos cahiers? Nous les achetons au petit magasin près de l'église. 7. Les livres de mon frère ne sont pas dans sa chambre. Où les cache-t-il? 8. Le cadeau de votre sœur n'est pas ici. Où l'a-t-elle caché? 9. Où est votre frère? Est-il malade? Non. Je l'ai vu hier. 10. Où sont les billets? Les avez-vous? Oui, je les ai.

Have a Try 9

Charles made the journey from London to Paris by aeroplane (by air). He is spending a week of his holidays in France with Jean, a French friend, who lives with his father and mother in a nice little house near the Bois de Boulogne. Yesterday Charles went for a long walk with Jean through the streets of Paris. After two hours' walk they looked for a café, and Charles, who is tired, is very happy to eat a nice vanilla ice while he watches the taxis and the cars which go by under the watchful gaze of a policeman (with) his white bâton in his hand.

Exercise 10 (*a*)

1. Among the animals in the Zoo there are two elephants and some tigers. 2. Who is that boy who has a pencil in the (his) hand? 3. The pencils which you have in the (your) hand belong to my brother. 4. Do you want some wine or some beer? 5. French wines are often very good. 6. We have bought some meat and some Italian cheese for our lunch. 7. The men (whom) you are looking at are American soldiers. 8. The young girls to whom you spoke yesterday are actresses. 9. The travellers who are getting into that bus have spent two days in our little town. 10. My aunt is very angry because the cheese which she has bought is not good.

Exercise 10 (*b*)

1. Il y a des agents de police devant le palais du roi. 2. Nous avons trouvé le petit chien que vous avez perdu hier. 3. Désirez-vous acheter des livres? Il y a un magasin près de l'église où nous les achetons quand nous avons de l'argent. 4. Les enfants qui regardent par la fenêtre de cette maison ne sont pas à l'école aujourd'hui, parce qu'ils sont malades. 5. Nous allons acheter du fromage et des pommes pour le déjeuner. 6. Le roi et la reine arrivent au château.

7. Il y a des livres qui ne sont pas trés intéressants. 8. L'actrice a perdu de l'argent, mais un agent de police l'a trouvé
dans une valise sous un lit à l'hôtel. 9. Les animaux qui sont
dans le champ sont des chevaux. 10. La maison que vous
regardez est au médecin.

Have a Try 10

Charles and Jean have taken the bus to go to Versailles.
The two boys found places on the platform at the back of
the bus, from where they looked with interest at the lively
streets of the town. After an hour's journey they arrive at
their destination and get out of the bus at the entrance to the
castle. "Of whom is that statue?" asks Charles. He points
to the large statue of a man on horseback. "That's the
king Louis XIV. He reigned longer than Queen Victoria.
At the beginning of his reign he lived in Paris, at the Louvre
—but at his orders an army of men worked to transform the
modest country house which existed here into the huge
castle which we are going to visit after lunch. There is a
restaurant near the castle where the meals are good and the
price reasonable."

Exercise 11 (a)

1. The house where I spent the holidays is situated (at)
fifteen kilometres from Paris. 2. My aunt lived for a long
time in that house which has a red door and a nice garden.
3. That little boy who ate seventeen green apples yesterday
is not at school today because he is ill. 4. Don't fall into the
water: it is very deep. 5. If you want to arrive at Versailles
before two o'clock, get into that bus. 6. The young girl
(whom) you are looking for is sitting at a table of (at) the
station café. 7. Among the travellers who are getting into
the three o'clock train for Paris there are fifteen American
soldiers, twelve Italian tourists and all the doctor's children.
8. If you go to the Zoo, buy some apples and some bread to

give to the animals. 9. All the windows of our house are
broken. I am sure that your little son has done it. 10. Where
is he? In the garden. Look. He has a brick in his (the)
hand.

Exercise 11 (b)

1. Regardez ces deux petites filles qui sont assises dans ce
bateau-là. 2. Traversons la rue pour monter dans cet
autobus-là. 3. Si vous désirez acheter des crayons rouges,
allez au petit magasin près du café. 4. Ne mangez pas cette
pomme-là: elle est verte. 5. Dans notre village il y a des
maisons qui sont faites de bois. 6. Il est onze heures, allons à
la gare. 7. Cherchez ma cousine: elle est assise sur une
chaise dans le jardin. 8. Nous avons des amis qui arrivent à
neuf heures de Londres. 9. Toutes les portes de l'église sont
fermées. 10. Il y a des agents de police qui cherchent partout
l'argent que le voleur a caché.

Have a Try 11

Charles and Jean have spent a pleasant hour sitting at a
table on the terraces of the café where they have had (taken)
their lunch. They are very content because the meal has
been excellent. At two o'clock they go into the castle and
begin to walk through the great galleries, where they admire
pictures of all sorts, painted (done) by celebrated artists—
portraits of historical figures, battle scenes. There are also
tables, chairs and sculptures which date from the age of
Louis XIV or his successors. After an hour the two boys go
into the great park of the palace, where there are long avenues
(which are) lined with trees and statues.

Jean looks at his watch. "Let us go and (to) buy some
postcards and also some fruit to eat during the return
journey."

Exercise 12 (*a*)

1. If these two children want to go to the cinema I will give them 4 francs (in order) to buy the tickets. 2. My brothers and their friends are not here, but if you go to the station I am sure that you will find them. 3. There is a letter for you on the table. 4. My father has sent me a postcard from London. 5. Yesterday I wrote him a long letter. 6. The present which I have bought is for her. 7. The two men to whom you spoke yesterday have been at school with me. 8. It is already three o'clock: let us go to the market without them. 9. The doctor's nephew and niece told me that he gave them twenty francs. 10. To whom do these two watches belong? This watch belongs to me, but the other belongs to him (is his).

Exercise 12 (*b*)

1. La vieille femme est très pauvre. Si j'ai de l'argent je lui donnerai cinq francs. 2. Si vous me donnez deux francs je porterai votre valise. 3. N'allez pas à l'hôtel sans lui. 4. Je lui ai envoyé une carte-postale. 5. Avez-vous écrit à vos neveux? Oui. Et nous leur avons envoyé un cadeau. 6. Notre chien est très intelligent. Quand je suis assis dans le jardin il m'apporte mon journal. 7. Où avez-vous été? Nous avons été au marché avec Jean et sa sœur. 8. Nos cousins sont très fâchés parce que nous ne désirons pas aller au cinéma avec eux. 9. Avez-vous vu l'agent de police? Oui, je lui ai dit qu'un voleur a pris ma montre. 10. Les garçons ne sont pas dans le jardin. Où les chercherons-nous?

Have a Try 12

A young boy, fifteen years old, made an expedition with his father into a region of India where there are all sorts of savage beasts. One day, while his father is away from the camp, this boy leaves his tent and begins to walk through the forest. Suddenly he hears grievous cries and finds in front of him an elephant which has a long thorn in his foot. The animal has so sad an air that the boy overcomes his terror. He tries to pull out the thorn, and after two or three vain efforts he performs this difficult and dangerous task.

Time passes, and the boy is now the father of a family. One day he decides to go to the circus in Paris. He does not have a very good seat among the spectators because he is not rich. An elephant comes into the ring and begins to do tricks. Suddenly the animal notices him and looks at him fixedly. He approaches him, lifts him in the air and puts him down on a chair in the first row. The elephant has a good memory!

Exercise 13 (*a*)

1. There are many men who have very little money. 2. How much French wine did you buy yesterday? 3. We bought two bottles of good white wine and some beer. 4. There are too many travellers in this compartment: let us get into another. 5. If you haven't enough money to buy the book which you want I will lend you 10 francs. 6. That man who is getting into the boat has drunk too much wine. I am sure he will fall into the water. 7. I have little cheese, but I have a small cake which is very good. 8. The weather is so fine today that I have spent two hours in the garden. 9. We spent very little time in the country, but we made three excursions by bus. 10. This little boy is ill today because he ate so many cakes and apples yesterday.

Exercise 13 (*b*)

1. Il n'y a pas assez de porteurs à cette gare. 2. Tous les œufs sont cassés parce que votre méchant neveu les a mis sur la chaise où sa tante est assise maintenant. 3. Au marché nous avons acheté du thé et une douzaine d'œufs.

4. Il y a une foule de touristes américains à l'hôtel. 5. Combien de valises avez-vous? Je suis sûr que le porteur les apportera à l'autobus. 6. Pourquoi désirez-vous monter dans un compartiment où il y a déjà une douzaine de voyageurs? 7. Il a bu déjà cinq tasses de thé et maintenant il a acheté une bouteille de vin rouge. 8. Je vous montrerai le livre que mon ami m'a prêté. 9. Nous ne passerons pas ici beaucoup de temps parce que nous désirons visiter l'église. 10. Nous n'avons pas beaucoup d'argent, mais nous vous prêterons deux francs pour acheter des gâteaux.

Have a Try 13

I found today in a Paris newspaper an article about a theft which has been committed at Lyons. A man telephoned to the owner of a big cinema and told him that some thieves are intending to enter this cinema at one o'clock in the morning. He assures the proprietor that he has telephoned to the police and that in five minutes some policemen will arrive at the cinema and will remain hidden inside to arrest the criminals at the right moment.

Five minutes after the proprietor lets in some men in police uniform. Their chief invites the proprietor to show him the safe where he has put the money which the spectators of the programme have paid to him during the day. The proprietor opens the safe to show that the money is untouched. The thieves, disguised as policemen, force the proprietor to give them the contents of the safe. They leave him in his office, his arms and feet bound with ropes and they go out cautiously into the deserted street.

Exercise 14 (a)

1. I have some things to buy in the market, but I will meet you at three o'clock at Jean's house. 2. There is someone at the door who wants to speak to you. 3. Your suitcases are very big: give them to the porter. 4. These vegetables are

not good: don't buy them. 5. Who is that officer whom we met yesterday at your aunt's house? 6. Our poor friend is very unhappy, because she has lost all her money. 7. To whom did you sell your old car? 8. Is there a good hotel in this town? 9. This morning I bought two kilogrammes of apples and six eggs. I will bring them to your house (home) this afternoon. 10. These little girls are very lazy: when they are at school they do not work.

Exercise 14 (b)

1. Y a-t-il de l'argent sur cette table près de la fenêtre? 2. Apportez-moi la valise que vous trouverez sous mon lit. 3. Nos amis sont maintenant à Paris. Envoyons-leur une carte-postale. 4. Il y a des œufs sur la table: ne les cassez pas. 5. Cet après-midi j'ai acheté trois kilogrammes de beurre chez Dupont. 6. Je cherche mon oncle, mais quelqu'un m'a dit qu'il n'est pas chez lui. 7. Où nous rencontrerez-vous? Je vous rencontrerai demain chez votre frère. 8. J'ai vu votre sœur ce matin. Pourquoi est-elle si malheureuse? 9. Pendant la nuit j'ai vu quelqu'un dans le jardin derrière la maison de vos amis: je suis sûr qu'ils ne sont pas chez eux. 10. Si vous n'avez pas perdu votre billet, donnez-le au porteur.

Have a Try 14

Yesterday (night) about eleven o'clock I looked out of my window, because my watch is not very accurate and I wanted to know if it is fast by comparing it with the church clock, which is near my home. At that moment I noticed to my surprise a man who is on the point of getting through a window into the house of my neighbour M. Leclerc. Without hesitation I telephoned to the police-station to report this incident. Soon some policemen arrive by car. They go cautiously up to the door of M. Leclerc's house. Someone opens it and they go inside. Five minutes afterwards they

leave the house and I am surprised to notice that M. Leclerc
is with them. It is evident that I have made a mistake. The
explanation is simple. When M. Leclerc arrives at his house
he finds that he has lost his key. His wife is spending two
days in the country at the home of some friends, and M.
Leclerc, whom I took for a thief, was forced to get into his
house through a window.

Exercise 15 (a)

1. Do you often go to the seaside? No, but when we
lived near Calais, I used to spend a lot of (much) time at the
seaside. 2. On getting into the train this morning, I saw our
neighbour who was talking to the porter. 3. We used to buy
vegetables in the market but now we buy them at Dupont's.
4. To whom does the big clock belong which you were
carrying when I met you yesterday? 5. That old woman
who is sitting at a table of (in) that café often used to give me
presents. 6. If we walk as far as the hotel I am sure that we
shall meet my neighbour; he is always there at this time (of
day). 7. My cousin used to work in a factory; now he is the
landlord of a hotel at the seaside. 8. Did you notice the
officer who was crossing the street while we were going to
the market this morning? 9. On arriving at the station I
bought two tickets. 10. If you walk with me as far as the
village I will show you the house where I used to live.

Exercise 15 (b)

1. Où alliez-vous quand je vous ai rencontré ce matin?
2. Je rencontrais souvent le médecin quand j'allais à l'école.
3. Ce petit garçon a acheté trois kilogrammes de pommes.
Lui avez-vous donné de l'argent hier? 4. En montant
(pendant que je montais) l'escalier, j'ai vu quelqu'un qui
entrait (allait) dans votre chambre. 5. Ma voisine n'est pas
chez elle. 6. Elle marchait vers la gare quand j'ai regardé
par ma fenêtre. 7. Hier nous avons fait une excursion à la

campagne. 8. Pendant l'après-midi nous avons passé deux heures dans les bois. 9. Nous passions nos vacances au bord de la mer, mais maintenant nous les passons chez ma tante. 10. Si vous ne travaillez pas pendant que vous êtes à l'école vous ne gagnerez jamais votre vie. 11. A l'école ce garçon-là ne travaillait jamais: mais maintenant il a plus d'argent que son père. 12. Nous la rencontrions souvent, mais quand nous allons à Paris elle n'est jamais chez elle.

Have a Try 15

At ten o'clock someone telephoned to the police station at Besançon to announce that thieves have taken out of (in) a postal van some sacks of letters and some parcels. The value of these parcels is at present uncertain, but it is probably great, because Besançon is famous for the excellence of the watches which are made in that town. Many watches are sent from Besançon to the shops of other towns in France, and it is certain that the thieves will find some watches in the parcels which they took.

Exercise 16 (a)

1. There were big trees and beautiful flowers in the garden of the house where we used to live. 2. If you have no money I will lend you five francs to buy some red wine. 3. While looking out of my window I saw an officer and a dozen French soldiers who were marching towards the station. 4. I am sure that they were going to get into the train which arrives here at three o'clock. 5. On getting into the bus I saw our neighbour who was buying green apples in the market. 6. I don't like green apples. One day I ate a kilogram of green apples and I spent two days in bed. 7. When we were small we often went to the seaside. 8. We used to spend our holidays at a farmer's house: he had no sheep, but he had some very fine cows. 9. I am sure that this man has drunk too much wine. He will fall into the river.

10. Have you a single room which looks (gives) on to the sea? No, madam, but we have a nice double room which looks on to the garden. 11. This place, madam, is taken (occupied), but there is a chair here which is free. 12. I have told you already M. Dupont, that I have no money to lend you.

Exercise 16 (b)

1. M. Vert et sa femme demeuraient dans notre maison. Un autre monsieur, M. Noir, était leur voisin. 2. Nous n'avions jamais de chiens quand nous étions jeunes (petits). 3. Nous demeurions dans une ville et il y avait beaucoup de voitures dans notre rue. 4. Mon oncle avait de beaux chevaux. Je les regardais pendant des heures. 5. Les chambres à deux lits sont occupées, madame, mais nous avons deux jolies chambres à un lit qui sont libres. 6. Les deux messieurs qui ont passé la nuit ici ont pris le train pour Paris ce matin. 7. Si vous ne désirez pas acheter ces journaux, mademoiselle, je les prêterai à Mlle Dupont. 8. Ce bon M. Dubois vous a apporté deux douzaines d'œufs et du vin blanc. 9. Il nous a dit qu'il n'avait pas d'argent, mais ce matin il achetait des légumes au marché. 10. Si vous marchez jusqu'à l'église vous rencontrerez M. et Mme Leclerc. 11. Il y a une foule d'enfants qui montent dans un petit bateau. 12. N'avez-vous pas assez d'argent français pour payer votre petit déjeuner?

Have a Try 16

The director of the business firm, where M. Lebrun, Jean's father, is employed, is ill. For this reason M. Lebrun has decided to go to Rouen in his place to discuss (speak of) an important matter with a client (customer) who lives in the old capital of Normandy. M. Lebrun has had the excellent idea of inviting his wife and the two boys, Charles and Jean, to go with him. Naturally Charles is happy to accept this

invitation, which will give him the opportunity to visit
Rouen, which is a very fine city and an industrial centre.

"There is a guide-book among the books which are on the
table near my bed," says Mme Lebrun. "I am sure that we
shall find in that book a list of the hotels at Rouen, and I will
telephone to the office of one of the hotels recommended in
my guide."

Exercise 17 (a)

1. If you are so ill, why did you walk as far as the old
castle? 2. We are going to visit Mme Dubois. If she is at
home I will invite her to dine with us at the hotel. 3. For
lunch yesterday we had fish and fruit. 4. This little boy
caught so enormous a fish that I thought (that) he would
fall into the water while he was pulling it to the surface.
5. Mme Leroux told me that she would lend me ten francs to
buy the tickets. 6. When the weather was fine we never
went (used to go) to the cinema. 7. If he did not want to go
to the seaside, why didn't he say so? 8. If all the places are
occupied we will get into another carriage. 9. That gentleman is a friend of my cousin. We met him at Mme Dupont's
(house). 10. I was not sure if you would arrive today or
tomorrow. 11. I told the doctor's son that he would not
earn his living if he did not work at school. 12. There is a
lady at the door who wishes to speak to (with) Mme Lepic.

Exercise 17 (b)

1. Vous trouverez de beaux poissons au marché ce matin.
2. Le marchand m'a dit qu'il n'a pas de légumes, mais il
nous apportera de grandes pommes. 3. Si j'avais assez
d'argent, je vous inviterais à dîner au "Cheval Blanc".
4. Cette vieille dame (-là) était une grande actrice. 5. Non,
madame, il n'y a pas de chambres à un lit qui donnent sur la
mer. 6. J'étais sûr que les agents de police n'attraperaient
pas les hommes qui ont volé (pris) votre voiture. 7. Si elle ne

désire pas aller au cinéma, donnez-moi son billet. 8. Si elle
est si riche, pourquoi ne donne-t-elle pas quinze francs à
son fils? 9. Ce poisson le tirera dans l'eau, s'il l'attrape.
10. Cette place est occupée déjà, monsieur. Si vous cherchez
vous trouverez une autre chaise qui est libre. 11. Combien
de vin rouge a-t-il bu? Trois bouteilles. 12. Nous n'étions
pas sûrs quand nous arriverions à l'hôtel. 13. Il ne manger-
ait pas tant, si je ne payais pas son dîner.

Have a Try 17

On getting out of the taxi, M. Lebrun looks anxiously at
the Station clock. "Good. We have ten minutes before the
departure of the train." He makes a sign to a porter, and
the four travellers give him their baggage. Charles notices
with interest that the porter fastens them to a strap which he
carries over (on) his shoulders.

"We are going to Rouen," says M. Lebrun, "by the eleven
o'clock train." "Yes, sir. If you go into the underground
passage I will look for you at the barrier."

At the booking-office M. Lebrun asks for four second-
class return tickets. They find their porter at the barrier.

"At this hour, sir, you will find places without difficulty."

In two minutes they are seated in a compartment where
there are no other passengers. Charles is very content
(pleased) because he has a corner seat. Mme Lebrun is not
so pleased. She looks at her husband reproachfully. "You
gave the porter too much money. Are we American
tourists?"

Exercise 18 (a)

1. With which knife did you cut the bread? With that
knife. 2. Where is my newspaper? Which newspaper?
The paper (which) I lent you yesterday. 3. There are already
fifty travellers sitting in the dining-room of this hotel.
Let us go and dine at home. 4. This author has written

forty-seven books. 5. The house where we used to live was at a distance of twenty-nine kilometres from Tours. 6. If you go to Tours you will find twelve or thirteen big castles at a little distance from the town. 7. I sent a postcard to my friend. He wrote me a letter of thirty-two pages 8. At what time shall we arrive in Paris? At three o'clock. 9. At what price did you buy that picture? I paid forty-two francs (for it). 10. What fruit do you prefer? I like apples (very) much. 11. How many boys are there in your class? There are thirty-seven (boys). 12. Have you a good place in your class (form)? Yes. Very good. I am sitting (I sit) near the window!

Exercise 18 (b)

1. Dans la salle à manger du vieux château la table est si grande qu'il y a des places pour quarante ou cinquante hommes. 2. Quels livres avez-vous pris? J'ai pris les deux qui étaient sur la table. 3. Cherchons votre ami. Dans quelle voiture est-il? 4. Quels livres préférez-vous? Je n'aime pas les livres qui sont très longs. 5. Le fermier m'a dit qu'il a acheté cinquante-sept vaches. 6. A quelle distance de Paris est votre maison? A trente-cinq kilomètres. 7. A quel hôtel dînerons-vous? Au "Cheval Noir". 8. L'auteur de ces livres que vous aimez était un de mes amis. 9. Je n'ai pas vu votre tante au café. A quelle table était-elle assise? 10. A quel hôtel avez-vous passé la nuit? Au "Grand Hôtel" qui a une douzaine de chambres à deux lits. 11. A quel prix avez-vous acheté les billets? A onze francs. Vous trouverez que nous avons de bonnes places. 12. Quel poisson avez-vous mangé? Je n'aime pas le poisson: nous préférons la viande.

Have a Try 18

For Charles the journey from Paris to Rouen was not long, because he spent the time in looking at the country.

He noticed that the fields in France are not separated one from the other by hedges, and that the women and the young girls help the men to grow vegetables or to guard the sheep.

When they arrive at the "Modern Hotel", situated in the centre of the town, the clerk (employee) at the office tells M. Lebrun that he has reserved him two double rooms, and he invites them to enter the lift. In reply to a question Mme Lebrun announces that she finds her room very nice. "And you, Jean?" "Oh, for me, meals have more importance than rooms!" "It is one o'clock," says M. Lebrun. "Let us go to the restaurant."

Exercise 19 (a)

1. Mme Leroux was not at home, but I met her in front of the church. 2. Where are the postcards which were on this table? I have given them to the doctor's little son. 3. I wanted some fish, but the shopkeeper has sent us some meat. 4. My newspapers are not here. Have you lent them to someone? 5. I am looking for my bicycle and do not find it. I am sure someone has taken it. 6. The soldiers were marching to the castle and we watched them for a long time. 7. This author has written many books but I have not read them. 8. That old gentleman and his wife live near us. I have seen them, but I have never spoken to them. 9. Where are your friends? Haven't you seen them? 10. My aunt is very angry. She bought some flowers yesterday and my dog has eaten them 11. If you don't like that lady, why did you invite her to dine? 12. Have you seen my shoes? Have you lost them? Should I look for them if I had found them?

Exercise 19 (b)

1. A quelle heure avez-vous rencontré votre tante? Je l'ai rencontrée dans la rue à quatre heures. 2. Ces souliers (-là) sont très grands. Où les avez-vous achetés? 3. Mme

Leroux est très fâchée parce que quelqu'un lui a envoyé de vieux poisson. 4. Je l'ai envoyé à Mme Leroux, parce que je ne l'aime pas. 5. Votre oncle et votre tante sont à Paris. Leur avez-vous écrit? 6. Où est votre bicyclette? Je l'ai mise derrière un arbre dans le jardin. 7. Où sont les fleurs qui étaient dans ma chambre? Je les ai perdues. 8. Pourquoi n'avez-vous pas invité vos cousins au dîner? Je ne les ai pas invités parce qu'ils ne nous ont pas donné de cadeaux. 9. J'ai trouvé des livres intéressants dans ce magasin près de l'église. 10. Je ne les ai pas achetés parce que je n'avais pas assez d'argent. 11. Nous ayions une voiture quand nous demeurions dans la campagne, mais nous l'avons vendue. 12. Etes-vous sûr que la porte est fermée? Oui, je l'ai fermée à huit heures.

Have a Try 19

At school Charles has had history lessons and his teacher has spoken to him of the life of Joan of Arc. In his history book also Charles has read with interest of this young girl who, under the inspiration of the saints who spoke to her, gave up the quiet life of her village of Domrémy to go and save France, desolated by the English invasion. She forces the English to abandon the siege of Orléans, but soon after this victory she falls into the hands of the Burgundians, who hand her over to their allies, the English, for an immense sum of money.

After their lunch at the "Modern Hotel" Charles and Jean visited the tower where Joan of Arc was imprisoned and the old Market Square where she was burnt.

Exercise 20 (a)

1. My cousin wanted to buy my old bicycle, but I had sold it already. 2. I was sure that someone had taken my shoes because I looked for them in all the rooms. 3. The shopkeeper was very angry because some naughty boys had thrown bricks in the street. 4. They had broken twelve

bottles of beer which he was going to send to the hotel.
5. I (have) told you that these shoes are mine: those belong
to the gentleman who is sitting at the table near the window.
6. I bought this book because it is more interesting than that
one. 7. There are ten people in that coach: let us get into
this one where we shall find some free (empty) seats. 8. We
have visited many castles, but we prefer this one because it is
more beautiful than all the others. 9. Which picture do you
prefer? This one or the one which I brought you? 10. We
were not sure in which train you would arrive—the two
o'clock (train) or the one which you took yesterday.
11. The green bicycle is not mine, but I will lend you this
one. 12. Where are your shoes? I have lost them: my cousin
has given me these.

Exercise 20 (b)

1. Qui était cette dame? Quelle dame? Celle qui regar-
dait les fleurs. 2. Dans quelle maison demeuriez-vous?
Dans celle-là. Elle a un joli jardin mais les chambres étaient
très petites. 3. De ces deux livres, nous préférons celui-ci,
parce que j'ai lu l'autre. 4. Montons dans cette voiture-ci:
il y a deux chiens et cinq enfants dans celle-là. 5. J'étais sûr
que je n'avais jamais vu cette vieille dame. Mais celle-ci qui
traverse la rue est une amie de ma tante. 6. Celle-ci est la
fenêtre qui est cassée: Regardez-la! 7. N'aviez-vous pas lu
dans le journal que la reine allait passer une semaine au
château? 8. Quel château? Celui que je vous ai montré
quand nous avons fait une excursion. 9. Il y a cinquante
personnes dans cet hôtel et toutes les tables sont occupées.
Non celle-ci est libre. 10. J'ai dit à ma sœur que je lui
avais écrit une longue lettre, mais elle ne l'a pas reçue.
11. Ces vaches-ci et celles-là sont à mon oncle. Nous avions
des vaches, mais nous les avons vendues. 12. Etes-vous le
méchant petit garçon qui a jeté cette brique-ci? Non,
madame, j'ai jeté celle-là!

Have a Try 20

Charles, who was tired, spent a good night. Jean and his mother are already in the hotel dining-room, and Charles arrives at the moment when the waiter brings the breakfast, which consists of a good cup of coffee or chocolate, with some bread and Norman(dy) butter. It is a less substantial meal than the English breakfast, but in France one has lunch an hour earlier than in England.

Exercise 21 (a)

1. I did not take your ten francs: it is that child there who found them. 2. If I had known that your friends were going to arrive by the ten o'clock train I would have met them at the station. 3. If you lend me two francs I shall have enough money (in order) to buy some fish and some fruit for lunch. 4. Who is that gentleman? He is John's uncle. It is he who bought our old car. 5. Who is that young man? That one? He is an American tourist. 6. What book are you buying? It is a book of the author whom we met at M. Leriche's (house). It is very interesting. 7. Look at those trees. We shall have some fine apples. 8. I should have had some beautiful fruit in my garden if your little nephew had not stolen it (them). 9. I do not like that gentleman. It is he who shut the door of the compartment at the moment when I wanted to get into the train. 10. Is it behind this tree that you put your bicycle? 11. I would have written to you if I had known in what hotel you were spending your holidays. 12. My aunt never travels by (in) plane: she thinks (that) it is dangerous.

Exercise 21 (b)

1. De ces deux tableaux c'est celui-ci que nous préférons. 2. Avez-vous assez d'argent pour acheter des légumes? 3. Avez-vous vu cette jeune dame. C'est la fille de notre

voisin. 4. Si j'avais su à quelle heure votre train arriverait je
n'aurais pas marché si vite à la gare. 5. Ce n'est pas à cet
hôtel-ci mais à celui-là que nous vous rencontrerons demain.
6. Est-ce lui ou sa sœur qui a gagné tous les prix? 7. C'est
un homme extraordinaire! Il a un avion et deux grandes
voitures, mais il voyage toujours à bicyclette. 8. Demain
pour notre petit déjeuner nous aurons des tasses de café avec
du pain et du beurre. 9. Ne montons pas dans ce comparti-
ment-là. Dans celui-ci il y a quatre places qui sont libres.
10. Ne marchez pas si près de l'eau. C'est dangereux.
11. C'est un médecin excellent, mais nous ne l'aimons pas
beaucoup. 12. Je ne travaillerai pas dans cette usine. J'aurais trop de travail.

Have a Try 21

While M. Lebrun is visiting a client, Jean and Charles are
on a walk in the town. Mme Lebrun has lent her guide to
her son and Charles has bought a plan of Rouen. They
arrive without difficulty at the Place Notre Dame where the
cathedral is situated. "Look at those two big towers," says
Jean. "This one is the St. Romain Tower and that one is the
Butter Tower." "Butter! Why? It's extraordinary." Jean
consults his guide book. "Ah, yes. The gentleman who
wrote this book gives us the explanation. In the good old
times it was forbidden to Catholics to eat butter in Lent, but
the bishop declared that the people who would give him
money for the building of this tower would have his permission to eat butter in Lent." "That's very interesting," says
Charles, "but if I was giving my money this tower would
have received the name of the 'Chocolate Tower'!"

Exercise 22 (a)

1. I have told you twice that I shall be at the market at
half-past two if the weather is fine. 2. Let us walk quickly,
we have not much time. It is already twenty (minutes) to

three. 3. The performance will begin at eight o'clock (in the
evening), but I will meet you in front of the theatre at a
quarter-past seven. 4. Excuse me, sir, what time is it,
please? 5. It is a quarter to nine, madam. Thank you (sir).
6. That young girl is very kind. I was going to get into that
train, but she told me that our train will not be here before
twenty-five past eleven. 7. It is five minutes to two by my
watch. We shall have time to buy some newspapers and
some postcards. 8. Walk more quickly, please. It will be
already midnight when we (shall) arrive at our house
(home). 9. In England we have lunch at one o'clock, but if
you spend your holidays in France you will have lunch at
noon. 10. If you get into this train you will be in Paris at a
quarter-past six. 11. I should have met them if I had known
at what time they would be at the station. 12. Is it noon
already? No. It is half-past eleven.

Exercise 22 (*b*)

1. Il est trois heures et demie. J'ai pensé qu'elle serait ici
avant deux heures. 2. Je l'ai vue deux fois, mais je ne lui ai
jamais parlé. 3. A quelle heure serez-vous à la gare? A
quatre heures moins quinze. 4. La représentation ne commencera pas avant huit heures et demie (du soir). 5. Si nous
arrivons au théâtre à huit heures moins vingt, nous aurons le
temps d'acheter des fruits et du chocolat. 6. Pardon,
monsieur. Quelle heure est-il, s'il vous plaît? Il est dix
heures vingt, madame. 7. Nous n'aurons pas assez de
temps pour visiter le château. Il est déjà midi moins dix.
8. Nous ne serons pas chez nous avant minuit si nous ne
marchons pas plus vite. 9. Quelle heure était-il quand vous
l'avez vue hier? Il était six heures moins dix. 10. J'ai pensé
que les magasins seraient fermés, parce qu'il était déjà cinq
heures et demie. 11. Combien de fois avez-vous été à Paris?
Trois ou quatre fois. C'est une belle ville. 12. Combien de
temps avez-vous passé chez le médecin? Nous étions chez
lui de trois heures jusqu'à quatre heures moins quinze.

Have a Try 22

At a quarter-past eleven Mme Lebrun and the two boys
are at the seaside. After breakfast they walked to the
station, where they took the express which brought them
in a very short time to Dieppe. There they get into one of
the buses which maintain the service (which run) between
Dieppe and Le Tréport, and they get out of the bus at a nice
little beach.

Jean and Charles look with satisfaction at the clear, calm
sea. In five minutes they are in bathing-dresses.

Jean points to a rock which breaks the surface of the
water at a distance of thirty metres. "I bet that I shall arrive
at that rock before you," he says.

The two boys begin to swim with all their strength
(might). The (his) head plunged in the water, Charles does
not notice an old gentleman in front of him and collides
violently with him. When he has apologised to him Jean is
already sitting on the rock.

Exercise 23 (*a*)

1. No, sir, Mme Dupont is not at home. She set out this
morning for the country. 2. If those little boys had not got
into that wretched little boat they would not have fallen into
the water. 3. Yesterday we went to Paris for the first time.
4. Our hotel is very large. We have a nice room on the
fourth floor. 5. She was going to spend her holidays at the
seaside, but she came back to Paris after five days. 6. At
school she used always to be (the) first in her class, but she
has become very lazy. 7. We made a nice excursion, but my
aunt, who was ill, remained in the hotel. 8. The landlord
went down to the cellar to look for a bottle of white wine.
9. If you had walked more quickly we should have arrived
home at lunch-time. 10. When I arrived at M. Dubois'
house, his sister told me that he had already set out for
Bordeaux. 11. It is the tenth day of our holidays. It is also

the ninth day of bad weather   12. She did not tell us that
she had come back by air (by aeroplane).

Exercise 23 (b)

1. A quelle heure est-elle arrivée chez vous? A minuit.
2. J'étais monté à ma chambre au septième étage. 3. Il est allé
à Paris mais se sœur est restée chez elle. 4. Nous sommes allés
(entrés) dans l'hôtel mais nos amis étaient partis déjà pour
le bord de la mer. 5. Nous demeurons dans la première
maison de la rue. Elle a une porte verte. 6. J'ai acheté
trois billets pour la deuxième représentation de ce soir.
Elle commence à huit heures et demie. 7. Nous ne serions
pas revenus si nous avions su que vous n'étiez pas chez vous.
8. Quand nous sommes arrivés à la gare le train était parti
déjà. 9. Les agents de police sont descendus à la cave où ils
ont trouvé deux jeunes voleurs qui étaient cachés derrière les
bouteilles. 10. Mme Dupont est très fâchée. Elle est montée
jusqu'au neuvième étage et en arrivant à sa porte elle a
trouvé qu'elle avait perdu sa clef. 11. Quand je l'ai vue pour
la première fois elle était jeune. Maintenant elle est devenue
très vieille. 12. Quand sont-ils revenus du bord de la mer?
Ils sont arrivés chez eux hier à sept heures et demie.

Have a Try 23

In Paris there are many houses which have no lift. For
this reason a person who occupies a flat on the first floor is in
general under the necessity of paying a higher rent than the
tenant of a flat on the sixth floor.

M. Billot was not rich, and that is why the flat where he
was passing his old age was on the seventh floor. The old
gentleman had in his room a grandfather clock. One day he
noticed with regret that the clock, which he liked very much,
was not going well. A clock-maker came to take the clock
away to repair it.

Five days later a man got out of a delivery van in front of

the house and began to climb the stairs, carrying the clock, which was now in good condition. At this moment a young man, who also lived in the house, saw the porter, who was coming up with difficulty because the big clock was very heavy.

"My friend," he said to him innocently, "if you want to know the time, why don't you wear (carry) a watch? It would be much simpler!"

Exercise 24 (*a*)

1. Which of these two bicycles belongs to you? This one belongs to me. 2. The gentleman to whom I sold my car has departed for the country. 3. To which of these gentlemen did you lend my newspaper? To that one. 4. The knife with which you have cut the bread is better than this one. 5. The rooms on the fifth floor are smaller than those on (of) the first, but they are less dear. 6. Of all the hotels in (of) this town the "Station Hotel" is the biggest, but at the "Black Horse" the meals are better. 7. Mme Chose is younger than my aunt, but she is much less pleasant. 8. There are fifty-five rooms in this hotel. Which is the one of your friends? 9. This author has written many books. Which do you prefer? 10. The landlord has given me two keys. Which is the one of your room? 11. I saw a thief who was getting through a window into one of these houses. But which? 12. Our neighbour is richer than we are; he travels first class, and in hotels he always has the best bedroom.

Exercise 24 (*b*)

1. Nous avons deux chambres qui sont libres. Laquelle préférez vous? 2. Dans laquelle de ces deux chambres avez-vous mis ma valise? Dans celle-là, madame. 3. A laquelle de ces filles avez-vous donné ma clef? 4. Auquel de ces deux garçons avez-vous prêté mon couteau? 5. Le château que nous avons visité hier est plus grand que celui-ci. 6. Si vous

allez à l'Hôtel de la Gare vous aurez une jolie chambre, mais ici les repas sont beaucoup meilleurs. 7. Nous avons vendu la maison dans laquelle nous demeurions. 8. Il y a beaucoup de cafés dans cette ville. Dans lequel est-il entré? 9. Le cheval est plus intelligent que le mouton, mais l'éléphant est le plus intelligent de tous les animaux. 10. De quel homme parliez-vous? Du médecin. 11. Duquel de ces deux messieurs parliez-vous? De celui-là. 12. La ville à laquelle il est allé est près de la mer.

Have a Try 24

"Where are you going to spend your holidays, my friend?" "In Paris. It will be my first visit." "In that case I advise you to lodge (put up) at a hotel near the Place St. Michel." "Why?" "Because in that part of the town there are hotels where you will find all the comfort which you want at a reasonable price." "Yes. But I should be (at) a considerable distance from the centre of Paris, and if I am forced to get into a taxi to go to the Cathedral, to the Louvre or to the big shops, I shall not have enough money to pay for my room at the hotel or (for) my meals in a restaurant." "(But) no, there is an excellent bus-service and you also have the Underground."

Exercise 25 (a)

1. The train is stopping because an old cow is sitting on the track: there are some travellers who are very annoyed! 2. On Monday the first of January we went to the theatre. 3. On Thursday the 28th of July we departed by air for France. 4. Don't cross the track at the moment when (where) a train is approaching. 5. The hunter has not killed the tiger. He has wounded it and the poor animal is hiding in the grass. 6. On the 5th of November the police(men) arrested many people who were throwing squibs in the street. 7. If you fall into this deep water you will kill your-

self. 8. From the 20th of August until the 6th of September I shall be at the seaside with my father. 9. When did you come back from Paris? We arrived home on Saturday, the 30th of July. 10. If you don't dress quickly you will have no breakfast. 11. If we hide in the cellar they will not find us. 12. If you are not careful you will wound yourself. Those big knives are dangerous.

Exercise 25 (b)

1. Si le train ne s'arrête pas à cette petite gare nous marcherons jusqu'à la ville. 2. Jeudi nous n'allons pas à l'école et nos vacances commenceront le quinze décembre. 3. Si vous jetez ces pétards vous blesserez quelqu'un. 4. Vous vous tuerez si vous n'êtes pas prudent. 5. Un mouton a été tué parce qu'il traversait la voie pendant que le train s'approchait. 6. Je suis sûr que ces garçons ne sont pas allés à l'école. Où se cachent-ils? 7. Le chien a caché le poisson dans le lit de ma tante. Elle sera très fâchée! 8. Vendredi le treize juin nous serons à Paris. 9. Nous nous habillons très vite quand nous sommes au bord de la mer. 10. Ma sœur est partie pour Londres le premier avril et elle est revenue ici le deux mai. 11. Pardon, madame. Les trains ne s'arrêtent pas ici. Cette gare est fermée. 12. Elle se blessera si elle n'est pas prudente.

Have a Try 25

"You told me that in Paris it is possible to go without difficulty by bus from the Place St. Michel, for instance, to the Place de l'Opéra." "Yes, it is very simple and, if you buy a booklet of tickets, you will find that it will be less dear than to buy a ticket each time that you get into a bus. If you go by (the) Underground it is possible to change train(s) once or twice and your ticket remains valid until you go up to the surface.

"At the entrance of a Métro station there is always a plan

which marks all the lines, and I am certain that you will have
no difficulty in finding if it is necessary or not to change in
order to arrive at your destination."

Exercise 26 (*a*)

1. While I was going down the stairs I met an American
tourist who was going up to the fourth floor. 2. This old
woman used to sell fruit and vegetables in (at) the market.
3. This old gentleman is very poor: if you do not want to
buy my old bicycle I will give it to him. 4. My friend will not
lend you his car because he has sold it to me. 5. This gentleman is very angry because he lent me his suitcase yesterday
and I have not given it back to him. 6. If you do not give
me back the money which you have stolen the policeman will
arrest you. 7. I wrote a long letter to my cousin, but I did
not send it to her. 8. Why? Because I hadn't any stamps.
9. I will lend you a franc to buy some stamps if you give it
me back this afternoon. 10. If you go down into the cellar
you will find some bottles of red wine which is very good.
11. Who gave them to you? It is my brother who gave them
to me. He received them from a friend. 12. If I had not
sold my car I would have lent it to you.

Exercise 26 (*b*)

1. Je lui donne de l'argent. 2. Il me vend des timbres-
poste. 3. Je les lui donne. 4. Il me les vend. 5. Je vous le
donnerai. 6. Nous la lui donnerons. 7. Je vous les montrerai. 8. Nous la leur vendions. 9. Il nous l'a prêté. 10. Il
vous l'a prêtée. 11. Je ne le lui ai pas envoyé. 12. Je ne la
leur ai pas envoyée.

Exercise 26 (*c*)

1. Si vous descendez à la salle à manger vous trouverez
des tasses sur la table. 2. Je lui ai prêté de l'argent, mais il ne

me l'a pas rendu. 3. Pourquoi ne vous l'a-t-il pas rendu?
4. Quelqu'un m'a vendu de très bons timbres-poste. 5. J'ai
une vieille bicyclette. Je vous la prêterai. 6. Je ne la lui
prêterai pas. 7. Pourquoi ne nous la prêterez-vous pas?
8. Si j'avais su que vous aviez lu ce livre je ne vous l'aurais
pas envoyé. 9. Ils nous l'auraient envoyé. 10. Ne vous les
a-t-il pas rendus?

Have a Try 26

One day a Norman farmer went to visit his neighbour who
was (a) coal merchant. "I have come to ask you a little
service (favour)," he says to him. "What service?" "It is a
question of the coal which I want to buy." "Yes. In those
sacks there is some coal which is very good. If, for instance,
you want ten sacks I sell them to you at ten francs the sack."
"That's dear enough," answers the farmer. "The little
service of which I spoke is that you sell me this coal at a
reduced price, because I am one of your best friends." "You
are asking me (for) something exceptional," answers the
merchant, "but since you are my friend I sell you this coal
at eight francs."

The farmer went away very pleased, but a month after he
came back. "This coal burns very quickly," he says. "I am
speaking of the coal which you sold to me at a reduced price
because I am one of your friends." "Ah, yes. I reduced the
price of the coal because you are one of my friends, but
because I am one of your friends I also reduced the quantity
of coal which I put in the sacks!"

Exercise 27 (a)

1. The men who were building a house in our street are
not working today. 2. If you do not finish your work you
will be punished. 3. On looking out of my window I saw an
old woman who was walking very slowly. 4. Of these two
books which do you choose? 5. Yesterday Mme Dupont

was choosing a present for her little daughter. She remained for a long time in the shop. 6. I had lent my bicycle to my neighbour. Fortunately he (has) returned it to me this morning. 7. Houses which are built of brick are better than those which are made of wood. 8. I was finishing my work when she came into my room. 9. You work very slowly. The others have already finished their work. 10. John's father never punished him when he was young. Now he is a very bad man whom the police arrested yesterday. 11. When we were young we always chose chocolate at breakfast; today we prefer coffee. 12. I don't much like this house which these men are building; it is less pretty than our neighbour's.

Exercise 27 (b)

1. Je choisissais des cartes postales dans un magasin près de l'église. 2. Je suis sûr qu'il travaillera bien si vous ne le punissez pas. 3. Notre voisin a acheté la maison qu'ils bâtissent. 4. Il y a des personnes qui marchent très lentement. 5. Je suis monté à sa chambre au cinquième étage mais il finissait son travail. 6. Des briques sont tombées de la maison qu'il bâtissait. 7. Heureusement j'ai trouvé le couteau que j'avais perdu. 8. La personne qui l'avait pris ne me l'avait pas rendu. 9. Ne punissez pas ce jeune homme. Pourquoi? C'est un voleur. 10. Ces cartes postales que vous choisissiez ne sont pas très jolies. 11. Je cherchais une vilaine carte postale. C'est pour mon frère. 12. Je vous ai acheté des timbres-poste. Lesquels choisissez vous?

Have a Try 27

The clients who put up at the "Hotel Splendide" are, in general, very rich. People who have not much money choose more modest hotels.

M. Dupuy, who was enormously rich, but of a far from

amiable disposition, always stayed at the Splendide when he
wanted to spend two or three days in Paris.

One morning at the moment when (where) he was coming
down from his room there was an electrical breakdown. In
consequence, the lift remained motionless. M. Dupuy, very
angry, made great efforts to open the door of the lift, but
without success. He is (a) prisoner. At this instant the small
son of one of the hotel maids was coming up the stairs. He
had been to the market, where his mother had sent him to
buy vegetables. This little boy did not like M. Dupuy, who
was a hateful man. He paid no attention to the cries of the
prisoner. For an instant he looks at the captive and, choosing a large carrot, he offers it to him. "Tiresome animal!"
he says. "I find you in a cage. Do you like carrots?"

Exercise 28 (a)

1. Who is this gentleman who has built this house? He is
a doctor. 2. He told me that he would sell me his knife, but
he has lost it. 3. What is that noise that I heard? What have
you done? 4. I was throwing bricks. You will find that the
dining-room window is broken. 5. Who is that lady, and
what did you say to her? 6. Whom were you waiting for
when I saw you this morning in the market-place? 7. If she
is not at the station at half-past six, I will not wait for her.
8. There are a crowd of people in front of the church. What
is happening? 9. I would punish him if he were more intelligent. He works well but he is the stupidest boy in (of)
the class. 10. Whom are you looking for? My cousin. She
told me that she would be here at midday (noon), but she
hasn't arrived. 11. What do you want to buy? Some
vegetables and some cheese. 12. Who told you that the two
o'clock train does not stop here? 13. What will happen if he
falls into this deep water?

Exercise 28 (b)

1. Qui attendez-vous? 2. Nous l'attendons. 3. Qu'avez-vous entendu? 4. J'ai entendu le bruit des hommes qui coupent les arbres. 5. Qu'a-t-il fait? Il a volé de l'argent. 6. Qui sont ces personnes à qui vous parliez? 7. Je ne suis pas sûr quand il bâtira sa maison. 8. Je vous vendrai du vin? 9. Si elle ne marche pas vite je ne l'attendrai pas. 10. Qu'est-ce qui arrivera si le train est parti déjà? 11. Que vendrez-vous? 12. Que vous a-t-elle dit? 13. Qui vous a dit que le train ne s'arrêtera pas ici? 14. Il y a toujours des places libres dans les trains qui s'arrêtent ici. 15. Qui est ce jeune homme que les agents de police ont arrêté? C'est le fils du fermier. 16. Ils ont fait tant de bruit que le propriétaire les a entendus. 17. Ces légumes sont très bons. Me les vendrez-vous? 18. Qui avez-vous rencontré ce matin? 19. Entendez-vous ces oiseaux-là? Je ne les entends pas. 20. Vous les entendriez, s'il y avait moins de bruit.

Have a Try 28

Mme Lebrun and the two boys were waiting for the arrival of the bus into which they were going to get in order to return to Dieppe. Among the crowd there was a man who, approaching a lady cautiously, took the large parcel which she was carrying under her arm.

"He's a thief!" cried Jean. "Let us go and look for him." "(But), no," said the lady, who, to the surprise of her travelling companions, has not the appearance (does not look) of being annoyed. "But we would have done our utmost to catch him, madam," says Jean. "Thank you," answered the lady, "but it will be the thief who will not be pleased. My poor little cat, who was very old, died yesterday. I occupy a flat in town, but I have a friend who has a nice garden. She promised to bury my cat, and it is this poor little animal which the thief will find in the parcel which he has taken."

Exercise 29 (*a*)

1. In this big plane there are places for one hundred and twenty-five people. 2. This plane has flown from Paris to New York in eight and a half hours—-a distance of three thousand miles or four thousand eight hundred kilometres. 3. I have lost your knife. Fortunately I have another which I will give you. 4. The king Louis XIV reigned for seventy two years. 5. He was King of France from 1643 until 1715. 6. We haven't any money, but my sister will lend you some. 7. Are you sure that she will wait for us? Yes. I am sure of it. She told me so twice. 8. That car which wounded a small boy while he was crossing the street was going too fast. 9. Yes. Much too fast. It was going at a speed of one hundred and five kilometres an hour. 10. How many houses are there in the street in which you live? There are ninety two. 11. Have you many stamps in your collection? I have fifteen hundred. 12. My uncle who has travelled much has sent me some stamps. I will give you a dozen of the best of them. 13. Thank you very much. You are very kind. I have some French books which I will lend you, if you haven't any. I have two or three which are very interesting. 14. Who is that author whom we met at the café? He is M. Vite. He has written one hundred and thirty-three books. I told him that I had read two of them.

Exercise 29 (*b*)

1. Un accident est arrivé au train. Trois voyageurs ont été tués et il y en a soixante-cinq qui sont blessés. 2. La Reine Victoria a régné pendant soixante-quatrè ans. 3. Elle était (a été) la Reine d'Angleterre de mil huit cent trente-sept jusqu'à mil neuf cent un. 4. Nous n'avons pas de chambres à deux lits au premier étage, madame, mais il y en a deux au troisième (étage). 5. Elles seront libres cet après-midi. En êtes-vous sûr? Oui, j'en suis sûr. 6. Je n'aurais pas acheté ces journaux si j'avais su que vous en

avez déjà trois. 7. La voiture dans laquelle nous étions montés allait à quatre-vingt-cinq kilomètres à l'heure. 8. Avez-vous entendu ce bruit pendant la nuit? Oui, j'en parlais au propriétaire. 9. J'ai fini ma lettre mais je n'ai pas de timbres-poste. En avez-vous? 10. Oui. J'en ai acheté une douzaine ce matin au café. Je vous en prêterai deux ou trois. 11. Marseille(s) est à une distance de huit cents kilomètres de Paris. 12. Je suis allé à Paris pour la première fois en mil neuf cent soixante et un.

Have a Try 29

1. The Government will examine the circumstances of the catastrophe to (of) the Calais to Paris train which came off the rails at the entrance to Abbeville station. This accident cost the life of the driver and of (to) thirteen travellers, and a hundred people were wounded (injured).

2. At Los Angeles the English (England) football team beat that of the United States by 8 goals to 1.

The team of Real Madrid has set out for Stuttgart, where it will meet the Rheims side in the final of the European Football Cup.

3. This month marks a victorious date for television. The first broadcast of television, intended simultaneously for several countries, took place in 1954. During seven days nineteen programmes were retransmitted and the Pope spoke in their native language to the viewers of eight countries. Eurovision which had transmitted the coronation of the Queen of England in 1953 has ceased to be a miracle.

Exercise 30 (a)

1. The poor little girl has killed herself in falling into the water. 2. If she had fallen into the water she would have killed herself. 3. Someone has told me that you were going to sell your house. Is it true? 4. I am looking for my two

brothers. Have you seen them? Where have they hidden themselves? 5. We dressed (ourselves) quickly because we were going to the seaside. 6. One often hears noises in this wood during the night. 7. During the sixteenth century they built some very fine castles in France. 8. Why did you go into this little shop? I was looking for some old books. One (you) find(s) some sometimes in these little shops. 9. If you had hidden yourselves in the wood they would not have found you. 10. It is true that people heard someone who was entering the hotel during the night. 11. We have been told (people have told us) that in the fifteenth century a general killed himself in one of the rooms in the palace. 12. Where is the tree in which King Charles II hid himself? It fell and they have cut it in pieces.

Exercise 30 (*b*)

1. On rencontre souvent des personnes qui ont été à Paris. 2. Est-il vrai qu'elle a gagné le premier prix? On me l'a dit. 3. La voiture ne s'est pas arrêtée. Les agents en ont arrêté le propriétaire. 4. Nous cherchions les garçons mais ils s'étaient cachés. 5. On a fermé la porte et je n'en ai pas la clef. 6. Les voleurs se sont blessés en entrant dans la maison par la fenêtre. 7. Cette bouteille ne s'est pas cassée! C'est lui qui l'a cassée. 8. Le grand livre qu'il avait jeté par la fenêtre est tombé sur la tête d'un agent de police. 9. Cette pauvre vieille femme s'est jetée sur la voie devant un train qui s'approchait. 10. Heureusement le train s'est arrêté, parce qu'il allait à une vitesse de vingt-cinq kilomètres à l'heure. 11. Pendant le dix-huitième siècle, si vous aviez pris un mouton ou quelquechose qui n'était pas à vous, on vous aurait tué. 12. Elle s'est habillée très vite, parce qu'elle allait rencontrer ses amis à sept heures et demie.

Have a Try 30

"Do you remember the French family whom we met when we were travelling in Normandy?" "Yes, very well. There were the father, the mother and two children." "Yes, that's right. They had already taken their places when we got into the train at Rouen, and I thought at the beginning that I was going to hate them." "I also (so did I). The weather was fine but the mother insisted that the windows remain shut." "Yes, but she was a very nice lady." "That's true. We hadn't enough money to go and lunch in the restaurant car." "No. We had bought in the station a small packet of chocolate." "Yes. And this admirable woman, who had brought bread, ham and fruit for the family's lunch invited us to eat some." "And we refused—out of politeness!" "Fortunately she insisted!" "Yes. I noted (down) all these details in my diary of the journey."

Exercise 31 (a)

1. Your sister is not very big. How old is she? She is fifteen. 2. I was ten years old when I went to the seaside for the first time. 3. Our house is smaller than yours, but we prefer ours because it has a very nice garden. 4. My car is this one; theirs is in front of the hotel. 5. She has lost her purse but I have found mine. Someone had put it on this table. 6. You are right; it is he who is wrong. 7. If you hadn't eaten so many green apples, you would not be seasick. 8. You will need all your money (in order) to buy this collection of postage stamps. 9. We have found our dog, but my friend is looking for hers. 10. Where is your naughty little nephew? He is never there when one needs him. 11. Your books are more interesting than ours but his (hers) are still better. 12. Your aunt and mine are forty years old, but my uncle is older than yours.

Exercise 31 (b)

1. J'ai huit ans. Jeudi mon père aura trente-neuf ans.
2. Quel âge avait-elle quand elle est venue passer ses vacances avec vous? Elle avait dix-sept ans. 3. Louis quatorze avait cinq ans quand il est devenu roi de France. 4. Il y a plus de moutons dans notre champ que dans le sien. 5. Il y a plus de fleurs dans notre chambre que dans la sienne. 6. Vous m'avez dit qu'il avait quatorze ans, mais vous aviez tort. 7. Si vous n'avez pas besoin de ces souliers, me les donnerez-vous? 8. Il m'a dit que mon frère et le sien étaient allés au cinéma. Avait-il raison? 9. La chambre dans laquelle le monsieur est entré n'est pas la sienne; on lui a donné une chambre au deuxième étage. 10. Quel âge a votre chien? Dimanche il aura quatorze ans. Et le vôtre? Oh, il est encore jeune. 11. J'avais perdu ma valise, mais ils m'ont prêté la leur qui est plus grande que la mienne. 12. Je vous donnerai mes souliers. Je n'en aurai pas besoin parce qu'ils sont devenus trop petits.

Have a Try 31

The time for (hour of) departure has come. "You have been very kind. Thank you a thousand times," says Charles to Mme Lebrun and Jean, who have accompanied him as far as the "Air France" office. An employee of the Company approaches a loud-speaker and announces: "The passengers by Air France bound for London are requested to get into the bus."

At eleven o'clock Charles and his travelling companions get out of the bus at Orly airport. The trip in the big plane—it is a "Caravelle" with seats for ninety-five passengers—lasts very little time. In reply to the question of a Customs Officer Charles declares that there are no cigars in his suitcase, and that he has no watches hidden in his pockets.

At the barrier he finds his mother, who has come to meet him.

"I am sure that you enjoyed yourself in France," she says
to him. "Do you speak French well now?"

"(But) no," answers Charles. "But I have made great
progress."

ALPHABETICAL WORD LIST

(Numerals, Days of the Week and Months are not included in this general vocabulary, since they are given in separate lists in the lessons concerned with them.)

A

à, to, at, in
acheter, to buy
accident (m.), accident
actrice (f.), actress
agent de police (m.), policeman
aimable, kind, nice
aimer, to like, love
aller, to go
américain, American
ami(e) (m.)(f.), friend
an (m.), year
anglais, English
Angleterre (f.), England
animal (m.), animal
après, after, afterwards
après-midi (m. or f.), afternoon
apporter, to bring
s'approcher (de), approach, to draw near (to)
arbre (m.), tree
argent (m.), money, silver
arrêter, to stop, to arrest
s'arrêter, to stop (oneself), come to a halt
arriver, to arrive
assez, enough, sufficient
assis, seated, sitting
attendre, to wait, to wait for
attraper, to catch
aujourd'hui, today
aussi, also
auteur (m.), author
autobus (m.), motorbus
autre, other
avant, before (of time)
avec, with
avion (m.), aeroplane
avoir, to have

B

bateau (m.), boat
bâtir, to build
beau, beautiful, fine
beaucoup, much, many
bête, stupid, (f.) beast
beurre (m.), butter
bicyclette (f.), bicycle
bien, well
bientôt, soon
bière (f.), beer
billet (m.), ticket
blanc(he), white
blesser, to wound
bois (m.), wood
bon, good
bord (m.), edge
bord de la mer, seaside
bottine (f.), boot
boulanger (m.), baker
bouteille (f.), bottle
brique (f.), brick
bruit (m.), noise
bu, drunk

C

cacher, to hide
cadeau (m.), present
café (m.), coffee, café
cage (f.), cage
cahier (m.), exercise-book, note-book
campagne (f.), country (as opposed to town)
carte (f.), map
carte-postale (f.), postcard
casser, to break
cave (f.), cellar
ce, this, that

celui, this (one), that (one)
cent, a hundred
certain, certain
chaise (f.), chair
chambre (f.), room, bedroom
champ (m.), field
chapeau (m.), hat
chasseur (m.), hunter
cher, dear
chercher, to seek, look for
cheval (m.), horse
cheveu (m.), hair
chez, to, at the house (home) of
chien (m.), dog
chocolat (m.), chocolate
choisir, to choose
chose (f.), thing
cinéma (m.), cinema
classe (f.), class, class-room
clef (f.), key
collection (f.), collection
combien?, how much (many)?
commencer, to begin
compartiment (m.), compartment
couper, to cut
courageux, courageous, brave
cousin(e) (m., f.), cousin
couteau (m.), knife
crayon (m.), pencil

D

dame (f.), lady
dans, in, into
de, from, of
déjà, already
déjeuner (m.), lunch
petit déjeuner, breakfast
demain, tomorrow
demeurer, to live, dwell
demi(e), half
derrière, behind
descendre, to go down, come down, put up at
désirer, to wish (to), want (to)
devant, before (of place), in front of

devenu, become
difficile, difficult
dîner (m.), dinner
dîner, to dine, have dinner
distance (f.), distance
dit, said, told
donner, to give
douzaine (f.), dozen
dur, hard

E

eau (f.), water
école (f.), school
écrit, written
église (f.), church
éléphant (m.), elephant
elle, she, her,
en, in, of it, some
enfant (m., f.), child
énorme, enormous
entendre, to hear
entre, between
entrer, to enter, go in
envoyer, to send
escalier (m.), stairs, staircase
et, and
étage (m.), floor
été, been
être, to be
eu, had
excursion (f.), excursion, outing
extraordinaire, extraordinary

F

fâché, cross, angry
fait, done, made
femme (f.), woman, wife
fenêtre (f.), window
fermer, to shut
fermier (m.), farmer
fermière (f.), farmer's wife
fille (f.), girl, daughter
fils (m.), son
finir, to finish
fleur (f.), flower
fleuve (m.), river

fois (f.), time(s)
franc (m.), franc
français, French
France (f.), France
frère (m.), brother
fromage (m.), cheese
fruit (m.), fruit

G

gagner, to earn, win, gain
garçon (m.), boy, waiter
gare (f.), (railway) station
gâteau (m.), cake
grand, big, great, tall
gris, grey

H

(s')habiller, to dress (oneself)
haut, high
heure (f.), hour, o'clock, time (of day)
histoire (f.), story, history
homme (m.), man
horloge (f.), clock
hôtel (m.), hotel

I

ici, here
intelligent, intelligent, clever
intéressant, interesting
italien, Italian
inviter (*à*), to invite (to)

J

jardin (m.), garden
Jean, John
jeter, to throw
jeune, young
joli, pretty, nice
jour (m.), day
journal (m.), newspaper
jusqu'à, until, as far as, up to

K

kilogramme (m.), kilogram(me)
kilomètre (m.), kilometre

L

là, there
lait (m.), milk
le (*la*), the
légume (m.), vegetable
lent(*ement*), slow(ly)
lequel, which (one)
lettre (f.), letter
libre, free, vacant
lit (m.), bed
livre (m.), book
Londres, London
long(*ue*), long
longtemps, (for) a long time
lu, read

M

madame, Madam, Mrs.
mademoiselle, miss
magasin (m.), shop
main (f.), hand
maintenant, now
mais, but
maison (f.), house
malade, ill
malheureux, unhappy
manger, to eat
marchand (m.), merchant, shop-keeper
marché (m.), market
marcher, to walk, to march
marée (f.), tide
matin (m.), morning
méchant, wicked, naughty, wretched
médecin (m.), doctor
meilleur, better
mer (f.), sea
merci, thank you
mère (f.), mother
midi (m.), midday
mille, thousand, a mile
mil, thousand (in dates)
minuit (m.), midnight
minute (f.), minute

mis, put
moins, less
moment (m.), moment
mon (*ma*), my
monde (m.), world
monter, to go up, get into
montre (f.), watch
montrer, to show
morceau (m.), piece, bit
mouton (m.), sheep, mutton

N

ne . . . jamais, never
ne . . . pas, not
neveu (m.), nephew
nez (m.), nose
nièce (f.), niece
noir, black
non, no
nuit (f.), night

O

occupé, occupied, taken
œuf (m.), egg
officier (m.), officer
oiseau (m.), bird
oncle (m.), uncle
ou, or
où, where
oui, yes

P

pain (m.), bread
palais (m.), palace
par, by, through, out of
parc (m.), park
parce que, because
pardon, excuse me
paresseux, lazy
parler, to speak
parmi, among
parti, departed, set out, started
partout, everywhere
passer, to pass, spend (of time)
pauvre, poor
payer, to pay, to pay for

pays (m.), country, district
pendant, during, for (time)
pendant que, while
penser, to think
perdu, lost
père (m.), father
personne (f.), a person
petit, small, little
peu, little, few
place (f.), place, square, seat
plus, more
poisson (m.), fish
pomme (f.), apple
porte (f.), door, gate
porte-monnaie (m.), purse
porter, to carry, to wear
porteur (m.), porter
pour, for, in order to
pourquoi, why
préférer, to prefer, like better
premier, first
près (*de*), near (to)
prêter, to lend
pris, taken
prix (m.), price, prize
profond, deep
propriétaire (m.), landlord, owner
prudent, prudent, careful
punir, to punish

Q

quand, when
qui, who, which
que, whom, which, that, than, what
quel, which, what
quelquechose, something
quelquefois, sometimes
quelqu'un, someone
qu'est-ce qui ? What?

R

rapide(ment), rapid(ly)
rapide (m.), fast train
reçu, received
regarder, to look at

régner, to reign
reine (f.), queen
remarquer, to notice
rencontrer, to meet
rendre, to render, give back
repas (m.), meal
représentation (f.), performance
rester, to stay, remain
revenu, come back, returned
roi (m.), king
rouge, red
rue (f.), street

S

salle à manger (f.), dining-room
sans, without
semaine (f.), week
si, if, so
siècle (m.), century
s'il vous plaît, (if you) please
situé, situated
sœur (f.), sister
soir (m.), evening
soldat (m.), soldier
soulier (m.), shoe
sous, under
souvent, often
su, known
sur, on
sûr, sure

T

table (f.), table
tableau (m.), picture
tant, so much
tante (f.), aunt
tasse (f.), cup
temps (m.), time, weather
tête (f.), head
thé (m.) tea
théâtre (m.), theatre
tigre (m.), tiger
timbre-poste (m.), stamp
tirer, to draw, drag, pull
tomber, to fall
touriste (m.), tourist

tout, all
train (m.), train
travail (m.), work
travailler, to work
traverser, to cross
très, very
triste(ment), sad(ly)
trouver, to find
tuer, to kill

U

un(e), a(an), one
usine (f.), factory
utile, useful

V

vacances (f. pl.), holidays
vache (f.), cow
valise (f.), suitcase, bag
vendre, to sell
venu, come
verre (m.), glass
vers, towards
vert, green
viande (f.), meat
vie (f.), life, living
vieux, old
vilain, ugly
village (m.), village
ville (f.), town
vin (m.), wine
visiter, to visit
visiteur (m.), visitor
vite, quickly
vitesse (f.), speed
voie (f.), (railway) track, line
voix (f.), voice
voisin(e),'neighbour, neighbouring
voiture (f.), (motor) car, (railway) coach
voler, to steal, to fly
voleur (m.), thief, robber
voyage (m.), journey
voyager, to travel
voyageur (m.), traveller
vrai, true
vu, seen